Vocabulary
Level 3
Table of Contents

Vocabulary Grade 3

INTRODUCTION

As students advance from grade to grade, word meaning becomes an important factor in comprehension since students encounter many unfamiliar words at these levels. When a student lacks a good meaning vocabulary, sentence comprehension and paragraph comprehension become difficult because of the many gaps in the continuity of the reading process.

It is important that the teacher build on the student's background of experiences as much as possible. The informational articles in this book have been selected to give the kind of direct and indirect experiences the student needs.

Throughout the book, new vocabulary words are introduced within the context of the articles. Students can use these context clues to determine the meaning of unfamiliar words. The use of context clues is often one of the easiest taught of the reading skills, and yet many students are unaware that it can be an effective method of deriving the meaning and/or pronunciation of words.

It has been accurately stated that the pen is mightier than the sword. The exercises in this book will help students make better use of their pens, and also their tongues, for they will develop their skill in using words effectively, both in writing and in speaking.

ORGANIZATION

Each of the five units focuses on specific curriculum areas: Health and Learning; Geography and Weather; Science and Technology; Plants and Animals; and Sports and Hobbies. Each unit contains five informational articles. Each article introduces eight vocabulary words. Following each article are two pages of word-building activities.

A focus on the second page of each lesson is using the words in a labeling activity. Further research may be necessary for the students to complete this activity. The activity pages also contain exercises that give students practice in figuring out the meaning of words. They include solving crossword puzzles, completing analogies, classifying words, finding synonyms, and matching words and meanings. The activity pages also contain suggestions for further exploration of the topic as well as suggestions for research projects and writing assignments.

USE

Vocabulary is designed for independent use by students. Copies of the activities can be given to individuals, pairs of students, or small groups for completion. They can also be used as a center activity.

To begin, determine the implementation that fits your students' needs and your classroom structure. The following plan suggests a format for this implementation.

1. **Explain** the purpose of the activities to your class.

2. **Review** the mechanics of how you want students to work with the exercises. Do you want to introduce the subject of each article? Do you want to tap into the students' prior knowledge of the subject, and have them create a word web?

3. **Do** a practice activity together. Review with students how to use context to figure out the meaning of a word. Remind them to use a dictionary when the context is not enough to figure out the meaning.

4. **Determine** how you will monitor the Assessment Test and Unit Reviews. Do you want to administer them to the whole class or to a group that has successfully completed a unit?

5. **Assure** students that all of the material is for practice purposes only. It is to help them improve their vocabulary.

ADDITIONAL NOTES

1. **Parent Communication.** Use the *Letter to Parents*, and encourage students to share the Letter to Students with their parents. Decide if you want to keep the activity pages and unit reviews in portfolios for conferencing or if you want students to take them home as they complete them.

2. **Bulletin Board.** Display selected research projects and writing assignments in your classroom. Encourage students to share the results of their research with classmates.

3. **Have fun.** Encourage students to create vocabulary games such as concentration and bingo that will give them practice using the vocabulary words.

Dear Parent:

A strong vocabulary is the key to success in reading and other school subjects as well as in speech and writing. Your child will be working on some practice materials to increase his or her vocabulary.

Using **Vocabulary**, we will read articles about many topics covering five themes. Vocabulary selected for study is presented in the articles. The articles are followed by activities to help your child learn word meanings and apply his or her understanding in a variety of ways. Your child may be assigned projects and writing assignments related to the topics. These assignments are planned to increase your child's vocabulary in reading, writing, and speaking.

Your child may bring home his or her folder of vocabulary activities. It is helpful if you and other family members talk about the work and share in the success of your child's achievement. Discuss the activities and the words learned. With your child, look for the words in print materials at home. Visit the library to get other books and videos on the topics the child has read and is interested in studying. This effort will encourage your child and promote learning throughout life.

Thank you for your help!

Sincerely,

—— Information, Please! ——

Read this information about using an encyclopedia. Think about the meanings of the words in bold type.

This vocabulary book is a treasury of information. As you do the activities, you will learn many new words. You will also read stories on many subjects, or **topics**. You will learn about cold deserts and meat-eating plants. You will discover what thunder is and why a dog growls.

Now suppose you want to learn more about a topic. Where will you look? The best place is in an **encyclopedia**. An encyclopedia has **facts** about people, places, and animals. It explains ideas and events in history. Some encyclopedias are made up of several books. Each book is called a **volume**. The topics in each volume are in **alphabetical** order. On the **spine**, or back edge, of each volume are guide letters. They tell you what topics are in that volume. There is also a number on the spine. The numbers help you put the volumes in order. Other encyclopedias are on **compact disks** or CDs. To use these encyclopedias, you need a computer.

No matter which encyclopedia you use, you find information in the same way. Suppose you need to answer the question, "What is a comet?" You can find the answer quickly by choosing a **key word**. In this question the key word is *comet*. You will find facts about comets in volume 2. If you're using a CD encyclopedia, you will enter the key word *comet* and double click on that name. An article about comets will appear on the screen.

Sometimes you need more than one key word to find information on a topic. Suppose you need to answer the question, "What is the difference between a star and a planet?" Here you must choose two key words—*star* and *planet*. You will find information about stars in volume 8. Information about planets is in volume 7. If you're using a CD encyclopedia, you will enter each key word separately.

Remember—using an encyclopedia is easy! All you need is practice.

A Picture Speaks Volumes!

| Edit | Create | **Identify** |

| **Label** |
| Estimate |
| Define |

Label each drawing with the correct vocabulary word.

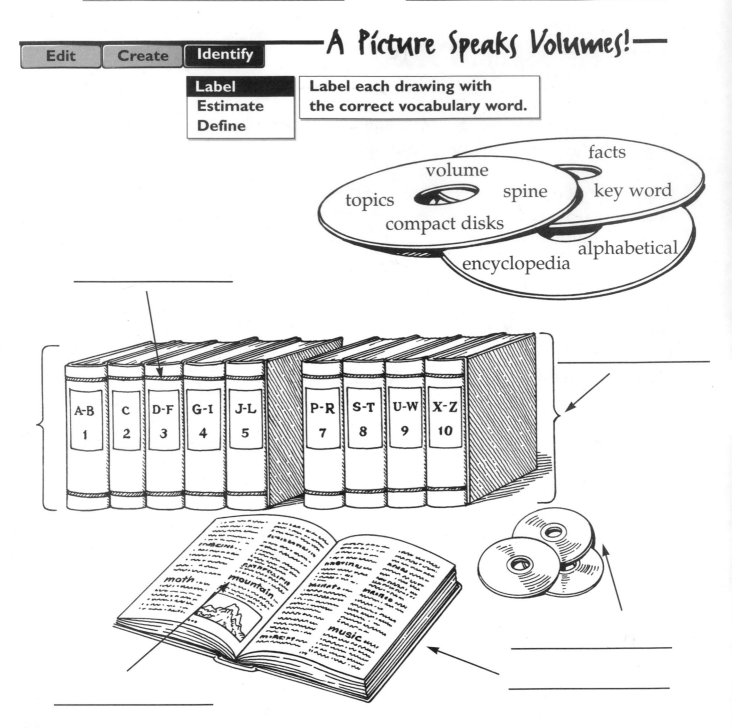

volume · facts · topics · spine · key word · compact disks · alphabetical · encyclopedia

A-B 1 · C 2 · D-F 3 · G-I 4 · J-L 5 · P-R 7 · S-T 8 · U-W 9 · X-Z 10

Also...

1. Draw a picture of something you would find in *volume* 8.

2. In which *volume* would you find *topics* beginning with the letter M?

3. Write the vocabulary words in *alphabetical* order.

Name _____   Date _____

Replace	Replace the word or
Classify	words in bold type with
Define	a vocabulary word.

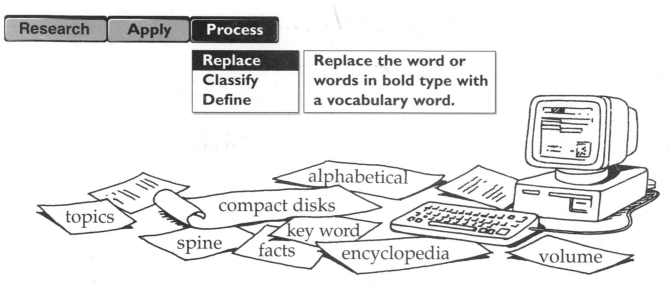

topics   compact disks   alphabetical   spine   key word   facts   encyclopedia   volume

This is KEY!

1. Our teacher wrote a list of **subjects** on the chalkboard.
   _____

2. He told us to find **things that have really happened** about one subject.
   _____

3. I went to the library to use the **set of books with articles on many subjects.**
   _____

4. The librarian helped me think of a **very important group of sounds having meaning** to use.
   _____

5. I found the first letter of the word on the **back edge of the book.**
   _____

6. That **one of a set of books** had all the information I needed.
   _____

Just the Facts, Please!

Imagine your local book store is having a contest. The grand prize is a CD encyclopedia. To win, you must write a paragraph telling why you want the disk. Use the words *alphabetical* and *compact disks* in your sentences.

Name _____   Date _____

Do I Have to Go to Bed?

Read this information about sleeping. Think about the meanings of the words in bold type.

"It's nine o'clock. Time to go to bed!" You've heard these words many times. Every time you hear them, your answer is **probably** the same, "Do I have to?"

What would happen if you stayed up all night? First of all you would feel tired and grouchy. You would find it hard to think and **concentrate**. You would not be able to pay attention at school. Also your **reactions** would be slow. If someone threw a ball at you, you might not be able to catch it.

How much sleep do you need? That **depends** on how old you are. Your body grows while you sleep. Babies grow fast. They need from sixteen to twenty hours of sleep every day. As they grow older, they need less and less sleep. Two-year-olds need about ten or twelve hours of sleep. They should also nap during the day. By the age of four or five, most children can do without naps. Teenagers need about seven or eight hours of sleep a night.

What happens during sleep? Your body's functions become less **active**. Your lungs breathe more slowly. You do not breathe as deeply as you do when you're awake. Your heartbeat becomes slower and more **regular**. Your muscles **relax** and need less blood. However, your body does not stay still. You move an arm or a leg or even turn over. You may do this thirty or more times each night. Your brain, too, becomes less active, but it does not shut down. It is busy going over the **events** of the day. It even tries to deal with problems. These activities take place while you're dreaming.

Though you may find it hard to go to bed, you can't do without sleep. It's an important part of your life. It's the time when you build up energy for the day ahead. So, tonight, sleep tight! Get ready for a new day!

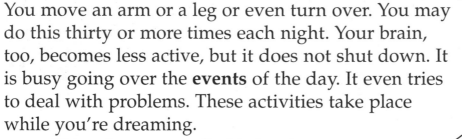

Don't Be Caught Napping!

| Edit | Create | **Identify** |

Label	**Label the drawing with the**
Estimate	**correct vocabulary words.**
Define	

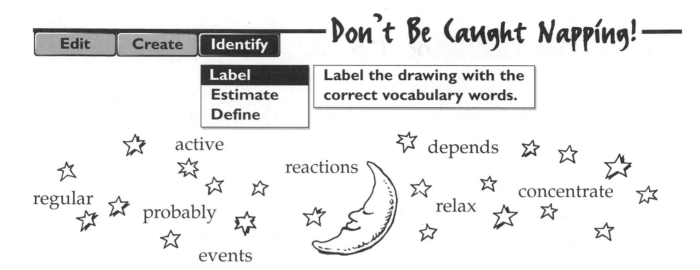

active   depends

reactions

regular   probably   relax   concentrate

events

_____

_____

_____

_____

Also...

1. Find a synonym for *probably*.
2. Find an antonym for *reactions*.
3. Draw a picture of something you do that is *regular* in your day.
4. Name something on which your happiness *depends*.

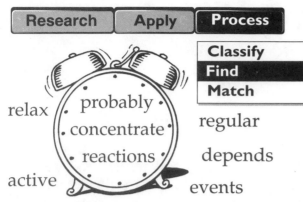

Research   Apply   **Process**

Classify
Find
Match

relax   probably   concentrate   reactions   active   regular   depends   events

Find the vocabulary word that fits each meaning. Write the word in the puzzle.

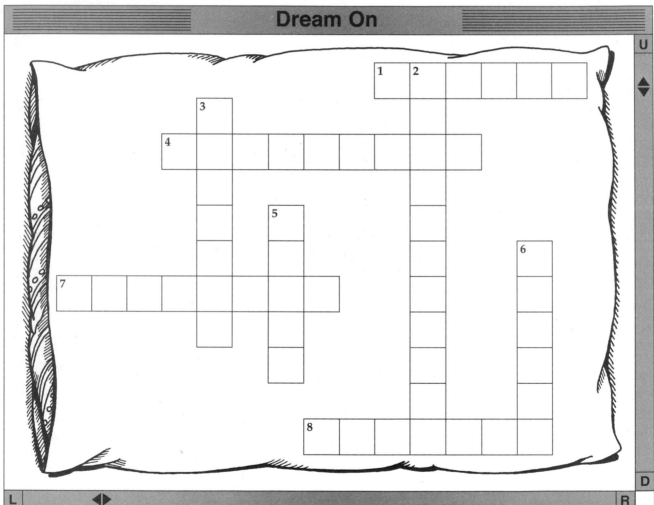

Dream On

ACROSS
1. busy
4. responses to things
7. most likely
8. determined by how something else turns out

DOWN
2. pay close attention
3. usual
5. become less tense
6. happenings

Hair I Am!

Read this information about hair. Think about the meanings of the words in bold type.

Look around the room at your classmates. Some have brown hair. Some have black hair. Some are blonde. One or two may be redheads. Some have curly hair. Some have straight hair. Some have long hair. Some have short hair.

What makes hair so different? Each hair on your head grows out of a tiny hole in your **scalp**. Below the scalp, each hair is in a bag-like structure called a **follicle**. A follicle can be round like a ball. It can be **oval** like an egg. It can be **narrow** like a little slot. Whether you have straight or curly hair depends on the shape of your follicles. If you are born with round follicles, your hair will be straight. If you have oval follicles, your hair will be wavy.

3rd Grade – Pinewood School

If you have narrow follicles, your hair will be curly.

Your hair gets its color from the **pigments** in the hair follicles. What are pigments? Artists add pigments to a liquid-like oil to make different colors of paint. The pigments they use are powders. While the pigments in your body are different, they act in the same way. Pigment is added to the hair **cells** as they form in the **root**. As you grow older, less and less pigment is added. So, over time, your hair will become gray or white.

If you're not happy with your hair, you can change it. You can color it with dyes. You can curl it with curlers. You can even straighten it. However, the changes will not be **permanent**. When new hair grows in, it will be the same as it was before you changed it!

Hair's to You!

Edit	Create	**Identify**

Label
Estimate
Define

Label the drawing with the correct vocabulary words.

follicle

scalp

narrow   oval

permanent

pigments

root   cells

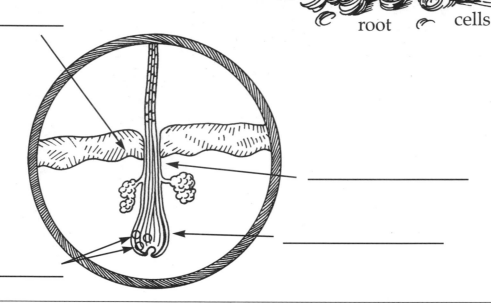

_____

_____

_____

_____

Also...

Classify the vocabulary words. Write the word that belongs in each group.

1. thin, skinny, _____

2. dyes, colors, _____

3. round, square, _____

4. lasting, remaining, _____

5. Draw a picture showing your own hair type.

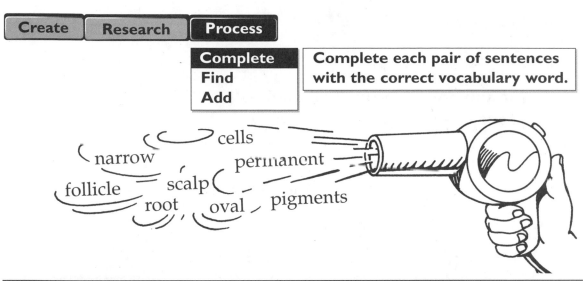

Create   Research   **Process**

Complete
Find
Add

Complete each pair of sentences with the correct vocabulary word.

A Hair-Raising Experience

U

1. The Mississippi River is wide.
   The Charles River is _____ .
2. A ball is round.
   An egg is _____ .
3. The top of a tree is the crown.
   The skin on the top of your head is your _____ .
4. You eat the leaf of a lettuce plant.
   You eat the _____ of a potato plant.
5. A tent is a temporary shelter.
   A house is a _____ shelter.
6. You can look at stars through a telescope.
   You can look at _____ through a microscope.
7. You add flour to water to make dough.
   You add _____ to oil to make paint.
8. A tulip grows from a bulb.
   A shaft of hair grows from a _____ .

D

L   ◄►   R

Permanent Waves

U
◄▼
D

Write two or three questions and answers about hair. Use as many vocabulary words as you can in your sentences.

L   ◄►   R

Name _____ Date _____

Excuse Me!

Read this information about some of the noises your body makes. Think about the meanings of the words in bold type.

You're taking a math test. The classroom is quiet, the way the teacher wants it. Suddenly you sneeze! *Aaaaah-Chooo!* You sneeze a second and a third time! *Aaaaah-Chooo! Aaaaah-Chooo!* The teacher glares at you. You try to stop sneezing, but you can't. Sneezes happen when something tickles, or **irritates**, the inside of your nose. **Mucus**, fluid that drips down from a stuffed-up nose, and dust can make you sneeze. **Pollen**, a yellowish powder that comes from plants, can also make you sneeze. When you sneeze, you suck in air. That's the *aaaaah* part. Then you blast the air out through your mouth. That's the *choo* part.

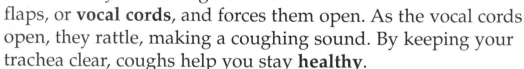

The dust and mucus that make you sneeze can also make you cough. When you cough, you breathe in deeply. The flaps at the top of your **trachea**, or main breathing tube, close. Pressure in your lungs builds up. Then the air blasts its way out through the closed flaps, or **vocal cords**, and forces them open. As the vocal cords open, they rattle, making a coughing sound. By keeping your trachea clear, coughs help you stay **healthy**.

Your body makes many other kinds of noises. It hiccups. It burps. It yawns. It snores. Your stomach growls. Your bones crack. Some noises come from the way your body digests food. Other noises are **signs** that your body is taking care of problems, like dust in your nose. No matter what the reason for a noise, you often can't **control** it. Just remember to say, "Excuse me!"

| Edit | Create | **Identify** | Something's in the Air... |

Label
Find
Match

Label the drawing with the correct vocabulary words.

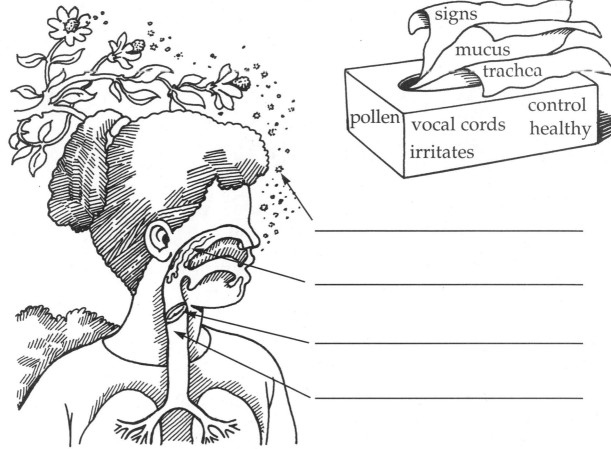

signs

mucus

trachea

pollen   vocal cords   control   healthy

irritates

_____

_____

_____

_____

Also...

Imagine that you are an editor for *TV Life Weekly*. Write the program note for a documentary on colds. Explain why viewers should watch the show. Use the vocabulary words *irritates*, *healthy*, *signs*, and *control* in your sentences.

TV *Life* WEEKLY   Jan. 23

FRIDAY LISTINGS
CONTINUED...

7:30

8:00   8:30

*Tonight at 8 on Channel 56
The Common Cold . . .
Discover what you and your
family can do to prevent it!*

Name _____   Date _____

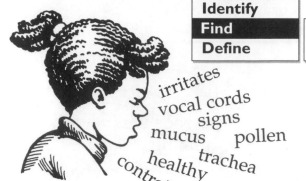

Identify
Find
Define

Find the vocabulary word
that fits each clue.

irritates
vocal cords
signs
mucus   pollen
trachea
healthy
control

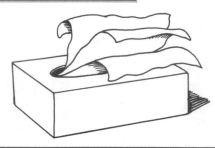

Cover Your Mouth!

_____ 1. free from disease or injury

_____ 2. main breathing tube

_____ 3. flaps moved by pressure

_____ 4. hold back or hold in

_____ 5. a yellowish powder that comes from plants

_____ 6. makes sore or sensitive

_____ 7. things that warn or point out what is to come

_____ 8. a slimy fluid that coats the inside of the nose

What Do You Say?!

Write the words in ABC order.

1. _____   5. _____

2. _____   6. _____

3. _____   7. _____

4. _____   8. _____

—— Have I Got an Itch! ——

Read this information about poison ivy. Think about the meanings of the words in bold type.

"Molly!" Jeremy calls his dog. "Stay out of there! The woods are full of **poison ivy**!" At the sound of his voice, Molly comes running. "Good girl," says Jeremy as he pats his pet. The pair head for home.

Later that evening, Jeremy notices a **rash** on the palms of his hands. It itches! "What's the matter?" his mother asks as she examines the rash. "This looks like poison ivy. Have you been playing in the woods?"

"No, Mom! I know what poison ivy looks like. I haven't been near it."

Jeremy is right. He didn't touch any poison ivy, but his dog, Molly, did. You can get poison ivy in two ways—**directly** or **indirectly**. You can get it directly by touching any part of the plant. You also can get it indirectly by patting an animal that has been in **contact** with the plant. The oily **substance** found in poison ivy plants can stick to a cat or a dog. It can also stick to clothes, to shoes, to a stick, or to a bicycle.

How can you **avoid** poison ivy? Remember the old rhyme, "Leaves of three, Let them be." The leaves of a poison ivy plant are dark green with saw-tooth edges. They grow in **clusters** of three. So if you find a plant with three leaves, don't touch it! And don't touch anyone or anything that has been in contact with it. Like Jeremy, you could get a rash!

Scratching for Words

Edit **Create** **Identify**

Label
Classify
Define

Label the drawing with the correct vocabulary word.

rash
avoid
contact
clusters
poison ivy
indirectly
directly
substance

Also...

1. Draw a picture showing something happening *directly*.

2. Write a sentence describing something happening *indirectly*.

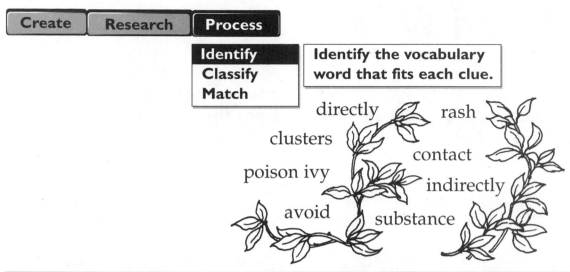

Create   Research   **Process**

Identify
Classify
Match

**Identify the vocabulary
word that fits each clue.**

directly   rash
clusters
contact
poison ivy
indirectly
avoid   substance

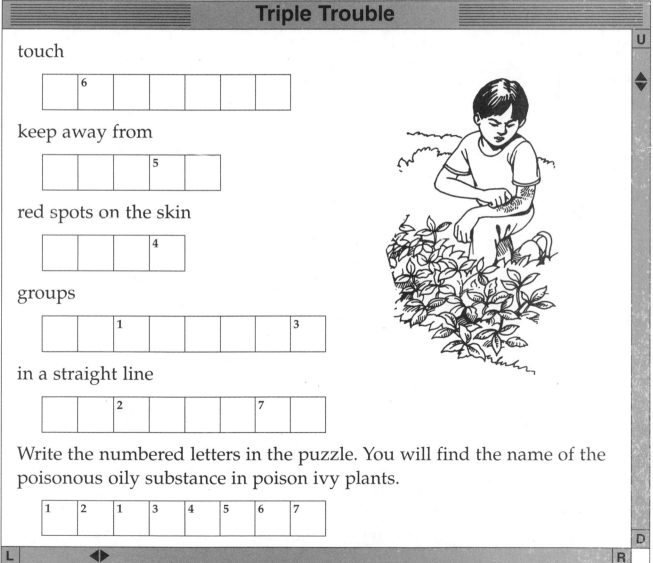

Triple Trouble

touch

	6				

keep away from

			5	

red spots on the skin

			4	

groups

	1					3	

in a straight line

	2				7	

Write the numbered letters in the puzzle. You will find the name of the poisonous oily substance in poison ivy plants.

1	2	1	3	4	5	6	7

Unit 1 Review

Antonyms are words that have opposite or nearly opposite meanings. Read these sentences. Choose an antonym from the word list for each word in bold type. Write it on the line. Read the sentence again to see if it makes more sense!

Word List

avoid	healthy	narrow	root	irritate
indirectly	relax	concentrate	permanent	contact

_____ 1. My little brother is **sick** and has lots of energy.

_____ 2. Our house is a **temporary** shelter.

_____ 3. He hurt me **directly** with his words.

_____ 4. The road through the mountain was **wide**.

_____ 5. He tried to **seek** trouble.

_____ 6. A cough can **soothe** a sore throat.

_____ 7. The evening is a great time to **work**.

_____ 8. She tried to **dodge** the ball with the bat.

_____ 9. The cat ran around the **crown** of the tree.

_____10. I try to **daydream** during a test.

Name _____   Date _____

The sentences on this page show how words that are alike can be compared. Read the sentences, and think about the meanings of the underlined words. Write the word that completes each sentence in the blank.

11. Numbers are to numerical as letters are to _____.
         order   alphabetical   group

12. Child is to backbone as book is to _____.
         spine   skeleton   bone

13. Running is to active as sit is to _____.
         sleep   watch   relax

14. Hardly is to never as maybe is to _____.
         probably   hopefully   if

15. Rectangle is to square as circle is to _____.
         round   oval   bowl

16. Milkweed pod is to seeds as flower is to _____.
         petals   pollen   stem

17. Clarinet is to reed as person is to _____.
         vocal cords   sing   play

18. Elephants are to herds as poison ivy is to _____.
         plants   itch   clusters

19. Butter is to toast as ointment is to _____.
         ill   rash   doctor

20. Set is to piece as encyclopedia is to _____.
         volume   read   learn

Are There Cold Deserts?

Read this information about deserts. Think about the meanings of the words in bold type.

After walking for miles, the man stumbles and falls. The sun beats down. Sweat covers his face and body. On his hands and knees, he slowly makes his way up the side of a **dune**. All around him are hills of sand. There are no trees nor bushes. There is no **vegetation** anywhere. "Water!" the man cries. "I need water!"

GREENLAND

You've probably watched this scene in a movie. Most people think all **deserts** are like this, but they're not. Some deserts don't have any sand at all. Some are actually cold. In fact, some are covered by a blanket of snow during part of the year.

What, then, is a desert? **Scientists** say that a desert is a place that gets very little **precipitation**. Precipitation can be in the form of rain or snow. What falls depends on the **temperature**. When it is warm, it rains. When it is cold, it snows.

You may not think of the **interior** of Greenland as a desert, but it is. Not much precipitation falls there. Yet, an **enormous** sheet of ice covers most of the island. In some places, the ice is almost a mile thick. How did the ice get so thick? The snow never melts. Even in the summer, the interior stays cold. The snow turns to ice. Year after year, the ice builds up.

The next time someone asks if you'd like to visit a desert, say, "No, thanks! I hate the cold!" Never mind if the person thinks you're crazy. You know the facts!

— Desert Trek —

Edit **Create** **Identify**

Label
Order
Find

Label the drawing with the correct vocabulary words.

deserts   dune
scientists
temperature
enormous   vegetation
precipitation
interior

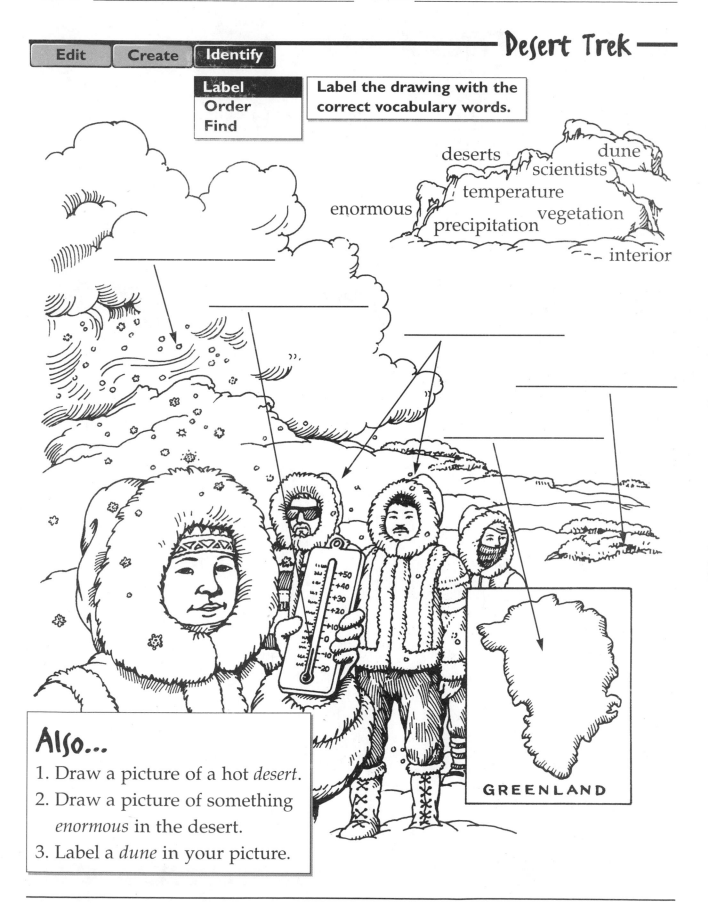

GREENLAND

Also...
1. Draw a picture of a hot *desert*.
2. Draw a picture of something *enormous* in the desert.
3. Label a *dune* in your picture.

Name _____ Date _____

interior
precipitation
temperature
vegetation
enormous
scientists
deserts
dune

Classify
Find
Define

Find the vocabulary word that fits each meaning.

ACROSS
1. 50 degrees, for example
3. very big
4. far from the coast
7. plants
8. dry places

DOWN
2. rain or snow
5. astronomers are these
6. a hill of sand

Think Thermals

Name _____ Date _____

What Will the Weather Be?

Read this information about weather forecasting. Think about the meanings of the words in bold type.

Will it be hot or cold? Will it rain? Will the sun shine? Knowing the **weather** is important to anyone who spends time outdoors. Farmers want to know the best time to plant. Sailors want to know about storms at sea. Skiers want to know if it will snow.

How did people long ago make **forecasts**? In ancient Greece Theophrastus (thee-oh-fras'-tuhs) wrote a book called *The Book of Signs*. In it, he listed over 200 signs of a change in weather. You know some of the signs. Grandma's bones ache. Your hair gets frizzy. These signs mean rain! People have used these signs for hundreds of years. Some people still use them.

Over time people found better ways to make forecasts. In 1643 Torricelli (tor-i-chel'-e) **invented** the **barometer**. This **instrument** measures the **pressure**, or force, of the air. With it scientists learned that air pressure changes. When it changes, the weather does, too. From then on, they began keeping records. Years later Ben Franklin studied the records. He figured out that storms move.

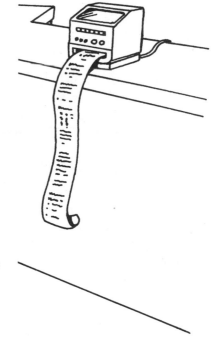

Knowing that storms move was a big step forward. Still scientists had to know where the storms were. How could they find out? They had to know what was happening in other places. In 1837 Samuel Morse invented the **telegraph**. Scientists used it to collect **information** from different places.

Over the years scientists have invented other instruments. Forecasts are getting better all the time. Do you really want to know if it will rain, Grandma? Forget your aches and pains. Listen to the weather report instead!

Name _____ Date _____

Edit   **Create**   **Identify**

Label
Replace
Add

Label the drawing with the correct vocabulary words.

invented
telegraph
forecasts
information
barometer
instrument
weather
pressure

"Today we'll see cloudy skies with a 40% chance of showers, and tomorrow we should start to see some more sun."

KGXO TV

Also...

Complete each pair of sentences with the correct vocabulary word.

1. Edmund Halley discovered a comet.

   Thomas Edison _____ the electric lamp.

2. Air temperature tells how hot or cold the air is.

   Air _____ tells how high or low the force of the air is.

3. Draw an *instrument* that you have used.

Create | **Apply** | **Process**

Label
Classify
Find

Classify the vocabulary words. Write the word that belongs in each group.

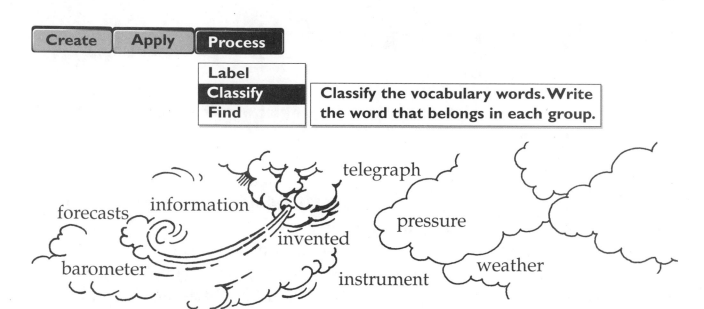

telegraph

forecasts information

pressure

invented

barometer

instrument weather

No Pressure!

1. wind vane, thermometer, _____

2. tool, utensil, _____

3. telephone, telegram, _____

4. facts, news, _____

5. land, climate, _____

6. made, created, _____

7. temperature, humidity, air _____

8. reports, predictions, _____

Key in to Weather

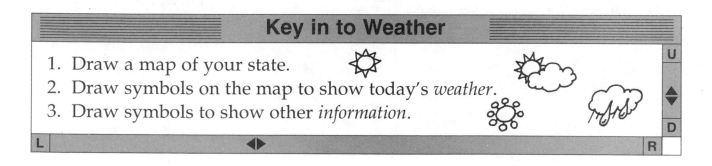

1. Draw a map of your state.
2. Draw symbols on the map to show today's *weather*.
3. Draw symbols to show other *information*.

Name _____ Date _____

In the Wake of Magellan!

Read this story about a great explorer. Think about the meanings of the words in bold type.

"Land ho!" the lookout calls from his perch high above the deck. He points to the **horizon**. The crew rush to the side of the ship. They see land! Nothing is more exciting after a long ocean **voyage**.

Ever since people began building boats, sailors have headed out to sea. Some went to look for riches. Some, like James Cook, went to **explore** new lands.

Cook was born in England on October 27, 1728. When he was 27 years old, he joined the Navy. He studied hard and learned to **navigate**. After he became a captain, he spent years **surveying** Canada's east coast. His **charts** were the best maps ever drawn of that coastline.

Then, in 1768, Cook led an **expedition** to Tahiti. The Navy asked him to take some scientists to the island. They also told him to look for an "unknown land" in the southern Pacific Ocean. At the time, many people believed a big **continent** was there.

While in Tahiti, Cook made friends with the people. He sent back reports telling about their way of life. Later he explored the coasts of New Zealand and Australia. He found no new continent because there was none!

In the following years, Cook went on 2 other expeditions. His voyages took him around the world a second time. He also traveled farther south than anyone had ever been. Then, in 1779, he was killed in a fight on Hawaii. With his death, England lost one of its greatest explorers.

Swab the Deck! —

| Edit | Create | **Identify** |

Label
Order
Define

Label the drawing with the correct vocabulary words.

horizon voyage charts
navigate expedition
surveying continent
explore

Also...

Find the vocabulary word that fits each clue.

1. The Titanic sank on its maiden one.
2. What George Washington spent his early years doing.
3. James Cook went on one to Tahiti.
4. Draw a picture of a place you would like to *explore*.

Name _____ Date _____

Create | Apply | Process

Identify
Match
Find

Identify the vocabulary
word that fits each meaning.

charts

expedition   continent

surveying   horizon   navigate

voyage   explore

Word Navigation

one of the seven large land areas on Earth

					4		

a journey by water

	7				

the line where the ground or the sea seems to meet the sky

					2	

to travel in unknown lands for the purpose of discovery

1						

measuring land to find out its boundaries, shape, or size

	8							

maps showing coasts, reefs, currents, and depths of the water

	5				

to steer a course in a ship

	6						

a journey made for a special reason

			3					

Write the numbered letters in the puzzle. You will discover the name
of the ship Cook sailed on his first expedition. Begin the word with a
capital letter.

1	2	3	4	5	6	7	8

Name _____   Date _____

Flash and Crash!

Read this information about lightning. Think about the meanings of the words in bold type.

Boom! You sit up in bed and look out the window. You see a flash of **lightning**. A few seconds later, you hear another loud crash. Again the lightning flashes. Heavy drops of rain beat against the window. Then just as suddenly as it began, the storm is over.

The bolt of lightning you see streaking through the sky is **electricity**. A single flash has about one billion **volts** of electricity. That's enough **energy** to keep a light bulb lit for three months.

When lightning flashes, it heats the air around it. The air gets hotter than the surface of the sun. As it heats up, the air stretches out, or **expands**. At the same time, it **vibrates**, or moves quickly back and forth. The sound that the air makes as it expands and vibrates is what we hear as **thunder**.

Thunder *always* follows lightning. You may not always hear it, however, because the storm may be far away. It's easy to figure out how far. Just count the seconds between the lightning flash and the thunder that follows. If you count to five, the storm is one mile away. If you count to ten, the storm is two miles away. How far away is the storm if you count to fifteen?

As you know, lightning can be **dangerous**. Every year in the United States, lightning sets off 10,000 forest fires. In the past fifty years, lightning has killed more than 8,000 people. So if you are outside during a thunderstorm, stay away from trees and anything made of metal. For the best protection, take cover! Lightning could strike!

Bright Ideas

Edit	Create	**Identify**

Label	Label each drawing with
Classisfy	the correct vocabulary word.
Order	

expands

thunder   energy   lightning

electricity

vibrates   volts

dangerous

BOOM!

Also...

1.   What is another word for *vibrates*?
2.   Draw a picture of something that *expands*.
3.   Draw three things from which you can get *energy*.

Name _____   Date _____

Research | Apply | **Process**

Identify
Find
Define

Find the vocabulary word
that fits each meaning.

lightning
thunder   energy
vibrates
expands   volts
electricity   dangerous

Get Charged

U

_____   1. a loud sound that follows a flash of lightning

_____   2. an important kind of energy that is found in nature

_____   3. likely to cause something bad or harmful to happen

_____   4. units that measure the force of an electric current

_____   5. a flash of light in the sky

_____   6. takes up more space

_____   7. power that can be used to do work

_____   8. moves quickly back and forth

D

L   ◆   R

Don't Be Shocked

U

Picture the words. Write two vocabulary words to show their meaning. Here is an example.

EXPANDS

D

L   ◆   R

Name _____   Date _____

Water World

Read the information about lakes. Think about the meanings of the words in bold type.

Where do you live? Do you live on the east coast of the United States? Do you live on the west coast? Do you live in the interior? No matter where you live, you may have visited a **lake**. If you haven't, you could visit one. There are thousands of lakes in the United States. They are everywhere. They are found in mountains and deserts, on plains, and near the shore.

What is a lake? A lake is a body of water **surrounded** by land. Lakes can be small or large. They can be deep or **shallow**. Small lakes are called **ponds**. Some lakes are so big they are called seas. The Caspian Sea is the largest lake in the world. The deepest is Lake Baykal in Russia. In places it is a mile deep.

How were lakes formed? All lakes fill **depressions**, or low places, in the Earth's surface. These depressions were formed in several ways. Many depressions were made by **glaciers**. As glaciers moved, these huge masses of ice carved out pits in the land. When the glaciers melted, water filled the depressions.

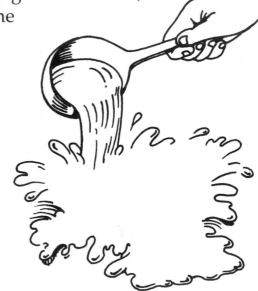

Some lakes form in the **craters** of volcanoes. When a volcano stops erupting, its crater may fill with water. Beavers make a lake when they dam a river. People also make lakes by damming rivers.

Lakes do not stay the same. They are always changing. Like people, they go through different stages. There are young lakes, middle-aged lakes, and old lakes. Slowly, lakes fill with plants and soil. Then they **disappear**.

Name _____   Date _____

Dipping into Words

Label
Classify
Define

Label the picture with the correct vocabulary words.

lake

glaciers
shallow   craters
depressions
ponds   surrounded
disappear

Also...

1. Write the word that means the opposite of deep.
2. Write the word that means the opposite of appear.
3. Draw something that is *surrounded* by water.

Name _____ Date _____

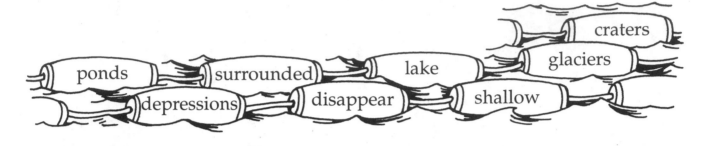

Edit   Create   **Process**

Find
Add
Complete   Complete each pair of sentences
with the correct vocabulary word.

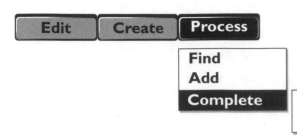

ponds   surrounded   lake   craters   glaciers
depressions   disappear   shallow

Sink or Swim

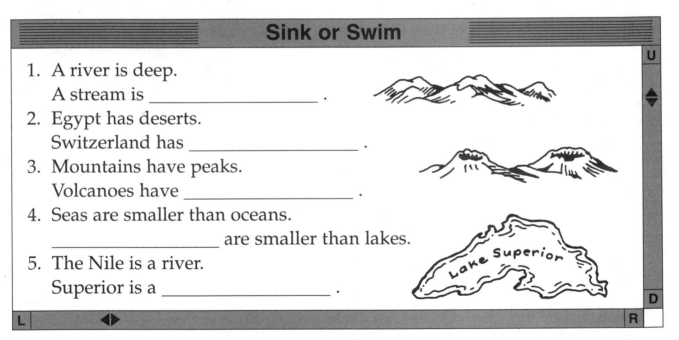

1. A river is deep.
   A stream is _____ .
2. Egypt has deserts.
   Switzerland has _____ .
3. Mountains have peaks.
   Volcanoes have _____ .
4. Seas are smaller than oceans.
   _____ are smaller than lakes.
5. The Nile is a river.
   Superior is a _____ .

Just the Tip of the Iceberg

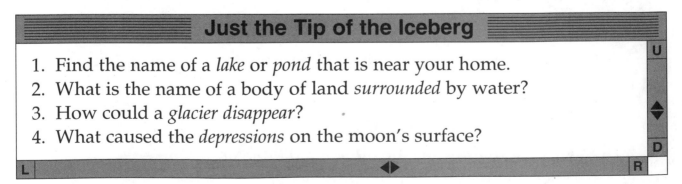

1. Find the name of a *lake* or *pond* that is near your home.
2. What is the name of a body of land *surrounded* by water?
3. How could a *glacier disappear*?
4. What caused the *depressions* on the moon's surface?

Unit 11 Review

Circle the word that has the same or similar meaning to the word or words in bold type. Read the sentence again, using your choice, to check your work.

1. The total amount of **water that falls as rain, snow, sleet, or hail** was above normal for the month.

    precipitation   thunder   vegetation

2. You can find **knowledge** and other facts about climate in an almanac.

    charts   forecasts   information

3. Alexander Graham Bell **made for the first time** the telephone.

    surrounded   invented   navigated

4. How many **units for measuring the force of an electric current** are there in an automobile battery?

    depressions   volts   craters

5. Long ago, **large masses of ice** covered large areas of North America.

    glaciers   deserts   continents

6. Lewis and Clark set out to **travel for the purpose of discovery** the U. S.

    vibrate   pressure   explore

7. Riding a bicycle without a helmet is **risky**.

    shallow   dangerous   enormous

8. Ancient paintings are on the **inside** walls of the cave.

    interior   expanding   pressure

9. The magician waved her wand and made the rabbit **pass out of sight**.

    expand   disappear   survey

10. The Pilgrims reached Massachusetts after a long **journey by ship**.

    expedition   horizon   voyage

Read each meaning. Fill in the bubble beside the word that fits the meaning.

11. **mound of sand**
    - ○ dune
    - ○ desert
    - ○ continent

12. **very large**
    - ○ expand
    - ○ enormous
    - ○ height

13. **find your way**
    - ○ disappear
    - ○ voyage
    - ○ navigate

14. **large land mass**
    - ○ continent
    - ○ glacier
    - ○ crater

15. **force**
    - ○ dangerous
    - ○ pressure
    - ○ expand

16. **a low area**
    - ○ interior
    - ○ depression
    - ○ continent

17. **the climate around us**
    - ○ weather
    - ○ electricity
    - ○ energy

18. **inside part**
    - ○ surrounded
    - ○ interior
    - ○ depression

19. **the plants of an area**
    - ○ charts
    - ○ forecasts
    - ○ vegetation

20. **maps showing information useful to sailors**
    - ○ charts
    - ○ information
    - ○ instruments

Name _____ Date _____

The Sky's the Limit!

Read the information about skyscrapers. Think about the meanings of the words in bold type.

Look at a photograph of Chicago's **skyline**. You will see a row of tall buildings. They are so tall they seem to scrape the sky. We call them **skyscrapers**.

About 150 years ago, there were no skyscrapers. Buildings were no more than 6 **stories** high. **Construction** workers knew how to build tall buildings. There were just no **elevators**. Imagine walking up 50 or a 100 flights of stairs. Then, in 1857, Elisha Graves Otis **designed** an elevator that could carry people safely. Elevators made taller buildings possible.

Chicago was the home of the first skyscraper. Built in 1883, the

Home Insurance Building was 10 stories high. It was the first building that had an iron and steel frame. Over the years, buildings got taller and taller. In 1895, the Park Row Building in New York City reached a **height** of 386 feet, or 29 stories. In 1931 the Empire State Building rose to a height of 1,250 feet or 102 stories. For years, it was the world's tallest building. Now the tallest building is the Sears Tower in Chicago. Built in 1974, it is 1,454 feet tall and has 110 stories.

How tall can a skyscraper be? A famous **architect**, Frank Lloyd Wright, drew plans for a mile-high building. That's 5,280 feet above the ground. It would cost about one trillion dollars. That's a lot of money! So far, no one can afford to build it!

Name _____ Date _____

| Edit | Create | **Identify** |

Label
Classify
Order

Label the drawing with the correct vocabulary words.

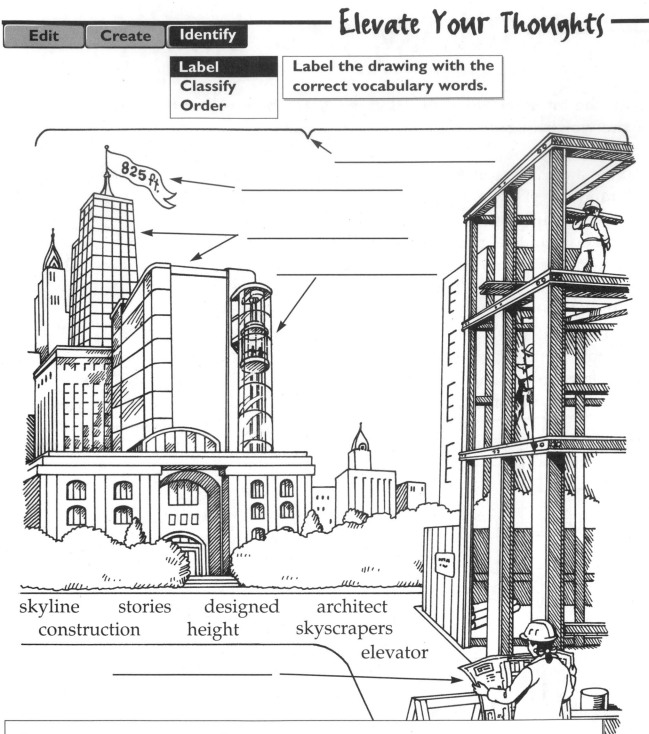

825 ft.

_____

_____

_____

_____

skyline   stories   designed   architect
construction   height   skyscrapers
elevator

_____

Also...

Imagine that a company is building a *skyscraper* in your city or town and needs workers. Write an ad for the Help Wanted section of the newspaper. Use the words *designed*, *stories*, and *construction* in your ad.

Name _____ Date _____

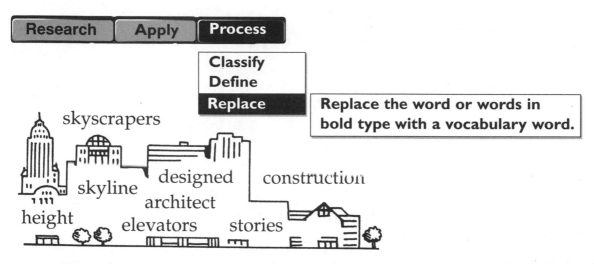

Research   Apply   **Process**

Classify
Define
Replace

Replace the word or words in bold type with a vocabulary word.

skyscrapers
skyline
designed   construction
architect
height   elevators   stories

Constructive Thinking

1. From the boat, we saw the **outline against the sky** of Chicago.

   _____

2. Mom took us to the top of one of the **tall buildings**.

   _____

3. We rode on one of the **little rooms that can be raised or lowered**.

   _____

4. The John Hancock Center was **planned** by Bruce Graham.

   _____

5. He is a talented **person who creates plans for buildings**.

   _____

6. The building is 100 **floor levels** tall.

   _____

7. It reaches a **distance upward** of 1,105 feet.

   _____

8. My grandpa was one of the **building** workers.

   _____

Build a Foundation

1. Draw a picture of the Empire State Building.
2. Write a caption that tells the *height* of the *skyscraper* and the number of *stories*.
3. Find the name of the *architect* who *designed* it.

Name _____   Date _____

Saturn, the Ringed Planet

Read the information about Saturn. Think about the meanings of the words in bold type.

Our sun has a family of nine **planets**. Of all the planets, many people think that the most interesting is Saturn. It is the sixth planet from the sun. Though it is far away from Earth, you can see it with your eyes. If you looked at it through a **telescope**, you would see bands of light yellow and gray.

After Jupiter, it is the biggest planet. It is so big that more than 800 Earths could fit inside it. As big as Saturn is, it doesn't weigh very much—for a planet. It is so light that it could float on water. Of course, you would have to find an ocean big enough to hold it. Unlike our own planet, its **surface** is not **solid**. Instead it is made up mostly of **gases**.

As you can see from the drawing, Saturn has rings. The rings are made up of **particles**, or pieces, of ice. Some of these pieces are the size of a speck of dust. Others are the size of a large building. Jupiter, Uranus, and Neptune also have rings, but theirs are not as big as Saturn's.

In addition to its rings, Saturn has at least twenty **moons**. That is more than any other planet. Titan is the biggest moon. In some ways it is like Earth. In 2004 scientists plan to land a **spacecraft** on Titan. Instruments will send information back to Earth. Scientists will study the information to learn more about Saturn's moon.

Name _____ Date _____

Edit	Create	Identify

Label
Order
Define

Label the drawing with the correct vocabulary words.

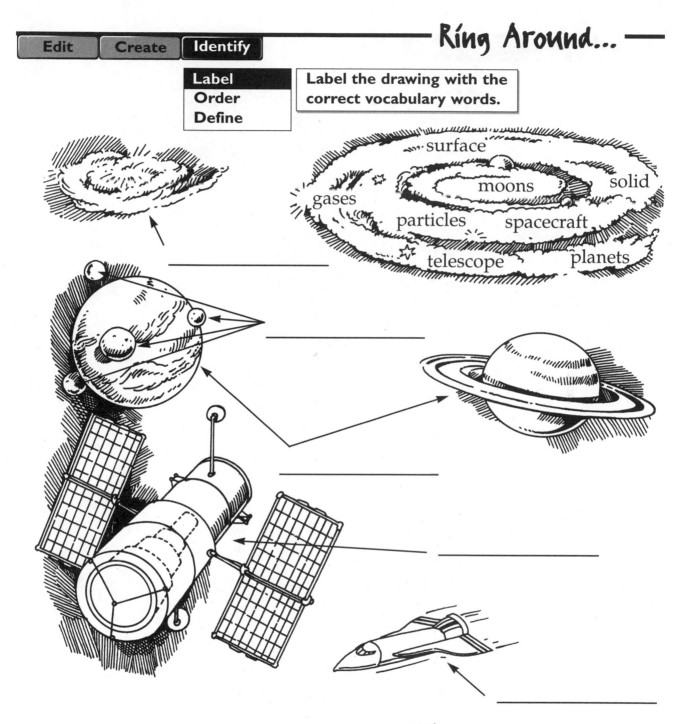

surface

moons

gases

solid

particles   spacecraft

telescope   planets

_____

_____

_____

_____

_____

Also...

Imagine you are on a *spacecraft*. Describe what you see as you circle the *planet* Saturn. Use the words *particles*, *surface*, and *solid* in your description.

Vocabulary 3, SV6767-0

Name _____ Date _____

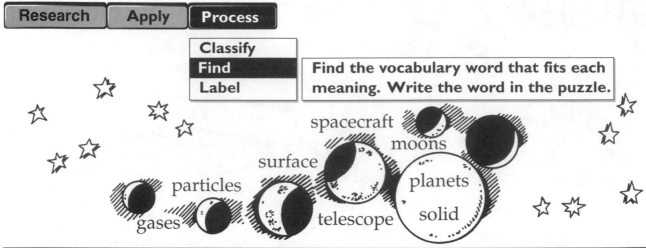

Research   Apply   Process

Classify
Find
Label

Find the vocabulary word that fits each meaning. Write the word in the puzzle.

spacecraft   moons
surface   planets
particles   solid
gases   telescope

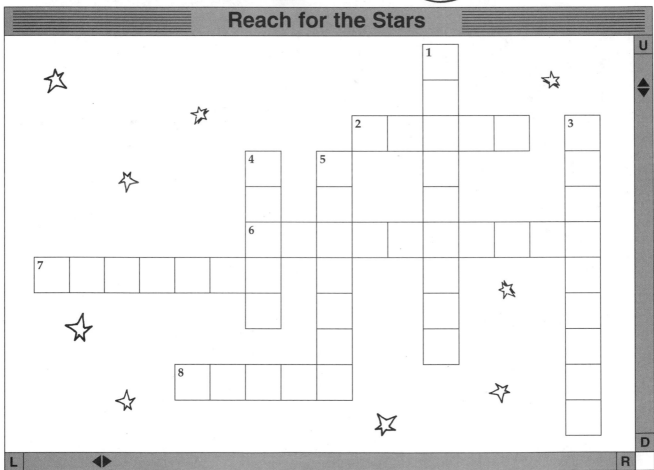

Reach for the Stars

ACROSS

2. hard

6. a vehicle that travels to outer space

7. the outside of something

8. Saturn has at least 20 of them

DOWN

1. an instrument for studying the stars

3. tiny bits of something

4. not liquids or solids

5. bodies that move around the sun

Name _____   Date _____

Let's Look at Television!

Read this information about television. Think about the meanings of the words in bold type.

When your grandparents were the age you are now, they didn't watch much **television**. Stations didn't start **broadcasting** shows until six o'clock. Until then, the only thing on the screen was a test **pattern**.

What is the story of television? It all started in 1837 with Samuel Morse's telegraph. This **device** sends messages over wires. Later, someone found a way to send pictures over wires. Then, in 1895, Guglielmo Marconi invented a new kind of **radio**. His radio didn't need wires. It sent sound through the air.

Soon people began to look for a way to send pictures over the air. It took years of hard work. In 1925, John Logie Baird found a way to do it. He used a device to break down a picture into lines. Another device sent the lines over the air to a **receiver**, or TV set. On the receiver, the lines once again formed the picture. Look closely at your TV screen. Can you see the lines?

At first, TV shows were just **still** pictures. The pictures didn't move, and they were in black and white. TV screens were small. Some were only 2 inches across. Over the years, television **improved**. Stations began broadcasting movies. Then they broadcasted "live" shows. Screens became larger. Now the shows are in color.

What's next? Now a picture on a TV screen has 525 lines. New screens will have twice as many lines. The pictures will be much clearer. Someday the pictures may even be 3-D!

Name _____   Date _____

| Edit | Create | Identify |

Label
Order
Find

Label the drawing with the correct vocabulary words.

television   radio

broadcasting

receiver   still

pattern

improved

device

radio

televison

Also...

1. Draw something that is the opposite of *still*.
2. Write how you think *television* could be *improved*.
3. Name something in your home that has a *receiver*.

Name _____ Date _____

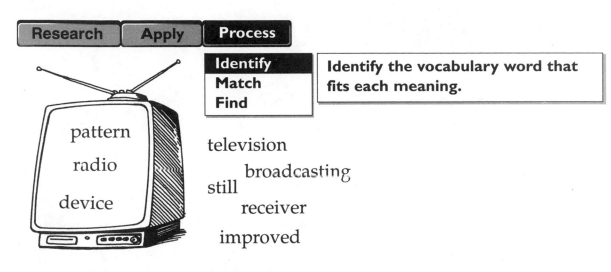

Identify
Match
Find

Identify the vocabulary word that fits each meaning.

pattern
radio
device

television
    broadcasting
still
    receiver
improved

Broadcast Your Knowledge

U

1. something that changes electric waves into pictures   _____

2. not moving   _____

3. something made for a special purpose   _____

4. a system for sending pictures and sound over long distances   _____

5. made better

6. a way of sending sound by electric waves   _____

7. sending out programs   _____

8. a design   _____

D

L   ◄►   R

You're On the Air

U

Write an ad for a *television* set. Use as many vocabulary words as you can in your sentences.

D

L   ◄►   R

Name _____ Date _____

Smooth as Glass

Read this information about glass. Think about the meanings of the words in bold type.

You pour your orange juice into it. You keep out the cold with it. You look at yourself in it. You can even see better with it. Glass is everywhere. Look around your house. List the things made of glass. Window panes, eyeglasses, light bulbs, mirrors, jars, bottles, the TV screen, vases, and the goldfish bowl are all made of glass. You may not see some things made of glass. **Fiberglass** fills the spaces behind the walls. This **material** is made of glass fibers, or threads. Fiberglass is a good **insulator**. It helps keep your house cool in summer and warm in winter.

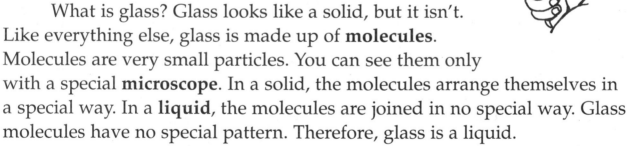

What is glass? Glass looks like a solid, but it isn't. Like everything else, glass is made up of **molecules**. Molecules are very small particles. You can see them only with a special **microscope**. In a solid, the molecules arrange themselves in a special way. In a **liquid**, the molecules are joined in no special way. Glass molecules have no special pattern. Therefore, glass is a liquid.

How do you make glass? It's really quite simple. The **ingredients** are cheap and easy to find. You need sand, soda, and lime. Soda makes the glass easy to melt and shape. Lime makes glass able to **resist**, or keep out, water. Without lime, glass would get soggy when filled with water. The sand gives it form.

Glass is amazing! It can be as hard as stone. It can be as soft as cotton candy. Every day, people are finding new uses for glass. Can you imagine a world without it?

It's Clear as Glass

Edit | Create | **Identify**

Label
Order
Find

Label the drawing with the correct vocabulary words.

molecules
fiberglass
material
insulator
microscope
ingredients
liquid
resist

Also...

Imagine you work for the Green Bottle Glass Company. Your job is to take visitors on a tour of the factory. What would you tell them about glass? Write your speech. Use the words *fiberglass*, *insulator*, and *resist* in your sentences.

Research   Apply   **Process**

Label
Classify
Find

Classify the vocabulary words. Write the word that belongs in each group.

insulator
liquid
resist

molecules
fiberglass
material
microscope
ingredients

Mirror, Mirror, on the Wall

1. gas, solid, _____

2. parts, contents, _____

3. atoms, particles, _____

4. cloth, fabric, _____

5. telescope, binoculars, _____

6. wood, metal, _____

7. cover, filler, _____

8. insist, consist, _____

Glass Act

List the *ingredients* of glass.

_____

_____

_____

Name _____ Date _____

Stuff It!

Read this information about a favorite toy. Think about the meanings of the words in bold type.

When you were younger, you owned at least one. You played with it. You took it to bed with you. You hugged it. You cuddled it when you were sick. What is it? It is a teddy bear. The teddy bear is the most **popular** stuffed animal in America. It was named for President Theodore (Teddy) Roosevelt. While on a hunting trip in 1902, he **spared** the life of a bear cub. When a toy maker heard the story, he made a stuffed bear. He called it Teddy's Bear.

Today toy makers still **manufacture** teddy bears. They also make many other stuffed animals. They make giraffes, panda bears, tigers, lions, and ducks. Some stuffed animals are small. Some are big. One manufacturer makes a bear that is so **huge** you could sit in its lap.

How do toy manufacturers make a stuffed animal? First, a metal pattern is made for each part of the animal—arms, legs, feet, and head. Next, each pattern is placed over a **fabric**. A **machine** pushes the pattern through the fabric like a big cookie cutter. A **tailor** sews the pieces together inside out so that the **seams** will not show. Then, another machine blows stuffing through a tiny hole in the seam. When a plastic nose and eyes are added, the stuffed animal often looks like the real thing.

The Bear Facts

| Edit | Create | **Identify** |

Label
Order
Find

Label the drawing with the correct vocabulary words.

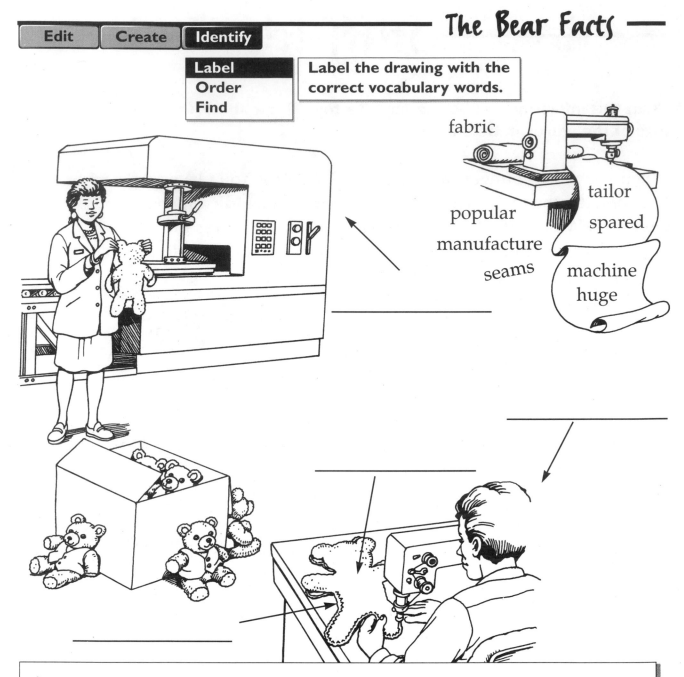

fabric

popular

manufacture

seams

tailor

spared

machine

huge

Also...

1. Draw a picture of a *huge* stuffed animal.
2. What is the most *popular* toy in your class? Ask your classmates to name their favorite toys. Make a chart showing the results of your survey.
3. Make a list of things that companies in your area *manufacture*.
4. Find a synonym for *spared*.

Name _____ Date _____

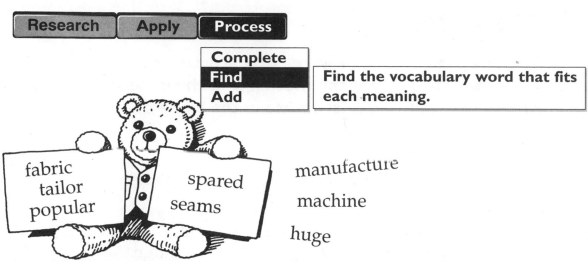

Research   Apply   **Process**

Complete
Find
Add

Find the vocabulary word that fits each meaning.

fabric
tailor
popular

spared
seams

manufacture

machine

huge

Piecing It Together

U

1. a material that is woven or knitted _____

2. very big _____

3. to make something _____

4. liked by many people _____

5. lines formed by sewing together
   pieces of cloth _____

6. a person whose job is sewing _____

7. a device that does some particular job _____

8. did not hurt or injure _____

D

L ◆▶ R

Sew What!?

U

Picture the words. Write two vocabulary words to show their meaning. Here is an example.

HUGE

D

L ◆▶ R

Unit III Review

The sentences on this page show how words that are alike can be compared. Read the sentences, and think about the meanings of the underlined words. Write the word that completes each sentence in the blank.

1. <u>Asia</u> is to <u>continent</u> as <u>Mars</u> is to _____ .
   skyline   telescope   planet

2. <u>Oxygen</u> is to <u>gas</u> as <u>water</u> is to _____ .
   solid   liquid   huge

3. <u>Thomas Edison</u> is to <u>inventor</u> as <u>Frank Lloyd Wright</u> is to _____ .
   popular   tailor   architect

4. <u>Barometer</u> is to <u>instrument</u> as <u>automobile</u> is to _____ .
   machine   gas   seams

5. <u>Sound</u> is to <u>radio</u> as <u>picture</u> is to _____ .
   microscope   television   receiver

6. <u>Bacteria</u> is to <u>microscope</u> as <u>star</u> is to_____ .
   pattern   receiver   telescope

7. <u>Hills</u> are to <u>mountains</u> as <u>buildings</u> are to _____ .
   skyscrapers   skyline   particles

8. <u>Ant</u> is to <u>tiny</u> as <u>elephant</u> is to_____ .
   solid   huge   still

9. <u>Little</u> is to <u>small</u> as <u>design</u> is to _____ .
   surface   insulator   pattern

10. <u>Silk</u> is to <u>fabric</u> as <u>fiberglass</u> is to _____ .
    insulator   improved   manufacture

Name _____ Date _____

Use words from the Word List to fill in the blanks of the story.

Word List

radio	huge	architect	surface	moon
designed	popular	resist	skyline	stories

A new building was built downtown. The idea for the new building was

created by a local **11.** _____ . She **12.** _____ it

to be new and exciting. Its theme is space. The **13.** _____ of

one of the walls has craters, like the surface of the **14.** _____ .

I heard all about it on the **15.** _____ , and I couldn't

16. _____ going downtown to see it. The front of the

building has **17.** _____ windows, and the area is

becoming a **18.** _____ attraction! I had heard a lot of

19. _____ about this new building. Now I can see that it will

really change the **20.** _____ of our city!

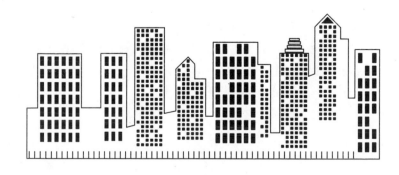

Grrrrrrrrrr!

Read this information about dogs. Think about the meanings of the words in bold type.

It's a lovely spring day. You go for a ride on your bike. Suddenly, you hear a barking sound. A dog starts chasing you. You pedal faster and faster. Luckily the dog gives up the chase. Whew! You had a narrow **escape**. Yet you did nothing to make the dog angry. Why did it chase you?

Like people, dogs can be **aggressive**. It's easy to tell when a dog is getting ready to attack. It barks! It growls! It snaps! It **lunges**, or moves forward suddenly! It bares its teeth! The question is, "What makes a dog act this way?" As you will **discover**, the answer is, "Lots of things."

Some dogs are very **possessive**. They don't want anyone near their food or toys. Some dogs become aggressive when someone enters their home or yard. These dogs "think" they are **protecting** their owners. Some **breeds**, like shelties and collies, are trained to herd animals. These dogs chase anything that moves. They run after squirrels and cats. They chase running children or moving bikes. Also, any dog who is afraid or hurt becomes aggressive.

Strange as it seems, a dog may "think" it is better than its owner. The dog looks upon its human family as its pack. In a pack, every member has a **rank**, or place. Most dogs have a lower rank than the human members. Sometimes, however, a dog may "think" it has a higher rank. It may even "think" of itself as being the pack leader.

You can teach a dog to obey you. You have to start early. The best time is when a puppy is between the ages of 4 and 16 weeks. Remember—it's up to you to help your dog be your best friend!

Dog Days

Edit	Create	**Identify**

Label
Classify
Order

Label the drawing with the correct vocabulary words.

possessive
lunges
escape
discover
protecting
breeds   rank   aggressive

GRRR

1ST   2ND   3rd

Also...

Write a list of suggestions for training and caring for a dog. Use the words *possessive*, *aggressive*, and *lunges* in your sentences.

Name _____   Date _____

Replace
Classify
Define

Replace the word in bold type with a vocabulary word.

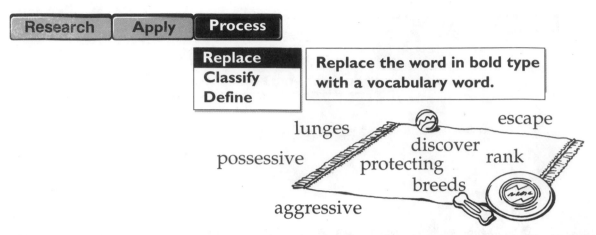

lunges   escape
possessive   discover   rank
protecting
breeds
aggressive

Leader of the Pack

1. Collies and poodles are popular **kinds** of dogs. _____

2. Labrador retrievers also **rate** high with people. _____

3. My dog is very **selfish** about his toys. _____

4. Sam is not **fierce** though. _____

5. Yet, he is always **defending** me. _____

6. When I throw a ball, my pet **jumps** for it. _____

7. Once Sam tried to **flee** from the yard. _____

8. I never did **learn** why he wanted to run away. _____

A Breed Apart

Complete the chart with facts about 3 different breeds of dogs.

Breed	Average Weight	Appearance	Characteristics

Name _____ Date _____

— All Beauty and No Brains —

Read this information about jellyfish. Think about the meanings of the words in bold type.

If you've ever been to the ocean, you've seen them. They look like milky white globs. What are they? They're moon jellies. Look closely. They have a **design** that looks like a cloverleaf on top. If the cloverleaf is white, the jelly is a **female**. If the cloverleaf is pink, it's a male.

A moon jelly is one of the most **common** kinds of **jellyfish**. It's the jellyfish you are most likely to bump into while swimming. Unlike other kinds of jellyfish, moon jellies don't sting. You can hold them in your hand.

A jellyfish is a strange animal! It can't swim. Instead, it moves through the ocean by shooting water from its body. The body is shaped like a bell. In some jellyfish, the bell is less than an inch in **diameter**. Other jellyfish have a bell that is more than 6 feet across their centers. Jellyfish have no brains. They don't even have heads. They do have a mouth, however. It hangs down from the center of the bell. **Tentacles** hang down from the edges of the bell. They are long growths that look like pieces of string. Jellyfish use the tentacles to catch their food. They feed on **plankton**, tiny plants and animals, and other jellyfish.

Because some jellyfish sting, swimmers don't like them. Other **creatures** love them. Ocean sunfish and sea turtles feed on them. Young fish, like cod and haddock, protect themselves by hiding behind the jellyfishes' tentacles. As you can see, every animal has its fans—even one as strange as the jellyfish!

Name _____ Date _____

Take a Dive

| Edit | Create | Identify |

Label
Classify
Order

Label the drawing with the correct vocabulary words.

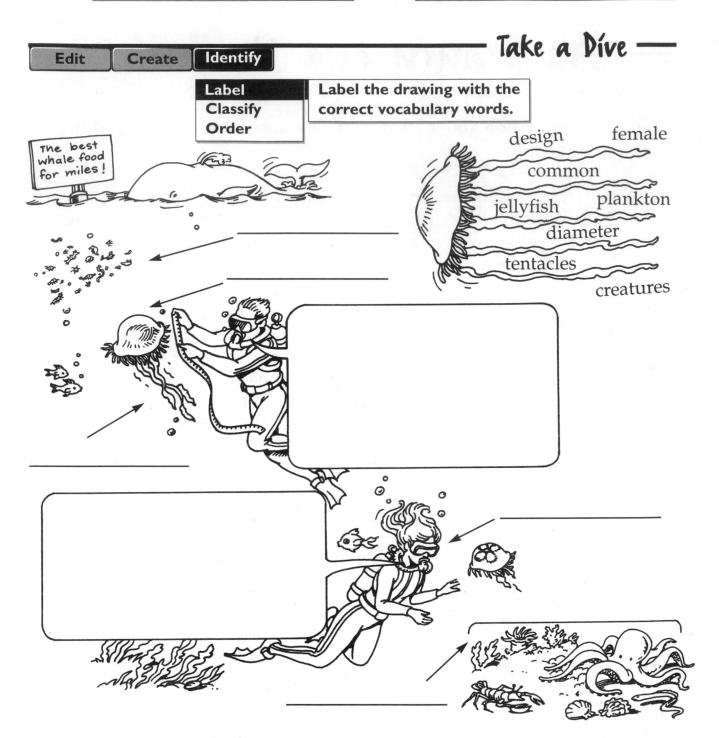

The best whale food for miles!

design   female

common

jellyfish   plankton

diameter

tentacles

creatures

Also...

Write what the scuba divers are saying. Use the words *common*, *diameter*, and *design* in your sentences.

Name _____ Date _____

Research   Apply   **Process**

Identify
Add
Match

Identify the vocabulary word that has the
same meaning as the word in each puzzle.
Write the word to complete each puzzle.

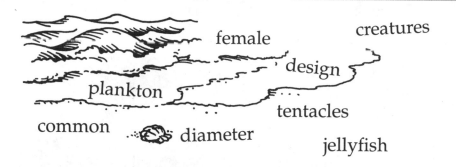

female   creatures

design

plankton

tentacles

common   diameter

jellyfish

Ocean Puzzles

1.
l
i
n
e

2.
w o m a n

3.
f
a
m
i
l
i
a
r

4.

p a t t e r n

Name _____ Date _____

Meat-Eating Plants

Read this information about some plants. Think about the meanings of the words in bold type.

A goat trots across a field. It stops beside some tall plants and begins to graze. Slowly a large leaf starts to reach out toward the animal. It covers the goat and then swallows it whole. Could this really happen? The answer is, "No!" No plant can swallow an animal as big as a goat. However, there are some plants that can eat small animals and **insects.**

The **marshes** of North and South Carolina are home to one of these animal-eating plants. In these low, wet lands grows the Venus flytrap. This plant has a snap trap. The trap works like a mouse trap with a spring. On the inside of each leaf are **sensitive** hairs. If anything touches them, they act quickly. When an insect brushes against the hairs, the leaf closes up. It traps the insect inside. Slowly the plant **digests**, or breaks down, the insect's soft parts. It leaves the hard parts "uneaten."

The horned bladderwort is another meat-eating plant. This plant has a **suction** trap. The trap works like a live animal trap. An animal can get in, but it can't get out. Small **sacs**, or bags, cover its leaves and **stalks**. Each sac has a **trapdoor**. Sensitive hairs grow around the trapdoor. When an insect brushes against the hairs, it is sucked through the trapdoor. Once inside, the insect is slowly digested.

You can grow these plants indoors. They need light and a lot of water. They will catch their own insects. You can also feed them a few small bugs each week.

Edit   Create   **Identify**

Label
Classify
Order

Label the drawing with the correct vocabulary words.

Don't Get Trapped!

insects   marshes   trapdoor

sacs   suction

digests   sensitive

stalks

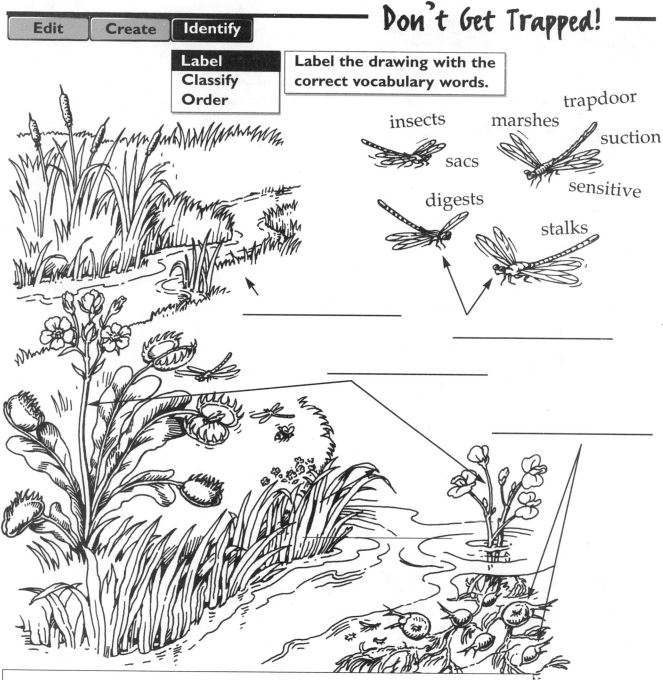

_____

_____

_____

Also...

1. Use a straw and a glass of water to demonstrate *suction*.

2. Draw a diagram to show how your body *digests* food.

3. Make a *trapdoor* in a piece of cardboard.

4. Explain why your skin is *sensitive* to the sun.

Name _____ Date _____

Classify
Find
Match

Find the vocabulary word that is described by each sentence.

stalks   insects

trapdoor   digests
sensitive   suction
marshes   sacs

Bug Off!

1. People don't want these at picnics. _____

2. Jack climbed one of these to get to the castle. _____

3. These are like swamps. _____

4. This is an opening in a floor or ceiling. _____

5. My brother is this, so he cries often. _____

6. These look like little bags. _____

7. This is what your body does with food. _____

8. A vacuum cleaner needs this to pick up dirt. _____

L ◆▶   R

Don't Feed the Plants!

Add one syllable from the first word to one syllable from the second word to make a vocabulary word. Write the word.

1. into + disects = _____

2. trappings + indoor = _____

3. direct + suggests = _____

4. succeed + nation = _____

L ◆▶   R

Name _____ Date _____

King of the Jungle

Read this information about elephants. Think about the meanings of the words in bold type.

Who is the "King of the **Jungle**?" You probably think it's a lion. The big cat certainly looks kingly. Other animals are afraid of it—and with good reason. Lions are great hunters. However, there is one animal that even a lion **fears**. That animal is the elephant. The elephant fears nothing.

Long ago there were about 350 kinds, or **species**, of elephants. They lived on every continent. Now only two kinds of elephants are left—the African elephant and the Asian, or Indian, elephant. The African elephant is the largest animal that lives on land. From trunk to tail, it is 25 feet (8 meters) long. It stands 13 feet (4 meters) high at the shoulders. It **weighs** more than 8 **tons** (8 metric tons). The Asian elephant is smaller. It is about 20 feet (6 meters) long and stands 10 feet (3 meters) high. It weighs "only" about 5 tons (5 metric tons).

Big animals have big **appetites**. In the wild, an **adult** eats from 400 to 600 pounds (180 kg to 270 kg) of food every day. It drinks about 40 gallons (150 liters) of water. It sucks up the water with its trunk. Then it squirts the water into its mouth.

Having a big trunk, or nose, is good for other reasons. An elephant has a very good **sense** of smell. Using its trunk and tusks, the animal can lift heavy loads. It can take the branches and bark off trees. It can even pull the tree out of the ground, roots and all. Finally, it can use its trunk to make a trumpet sound.

TA-DAHHHH! Imagine hearing that sound in the jungle. No wonder other animals dash off. Even a lion will sneak away into the bush.

Name _____ Date _____

| Edit | Create | **Identify** |

Label
Classify
Estimate

Label the drawing with the correct vocabulary words.

jungle
sense
weighs
adult
appetites
fears
species
tons

16,000 lbs

African Elephants

_____

_____

_____

_____

Also...

Imagine that an elephant and a lion could talk to one another. What would they say? Write a conversation between an elephant and a lion. Use the words *fears*, *appetites*, *weighs*, and *sense* in your sentences.

Name _____ Date _____

Research | Apply | **Process**

Identify
Find
Classify

Identify the vocabulary word
that fits each meaning.

jungle   fears
sense   tons
weighs   adult
appetites   species

Have No Fear!

a group of animals

	1					

an animal that is fully grown

			2	

what an animal uses to learn about its surroundings

		4		

finds out the heaviness of an animal

					6

is afraid of

		3		

desires for food

				5				

Write the numbered letters in the puzzle. You will find the answer
to the question, "What do elephants eat?"

1	2	3	4	5	6

Name _____   Date _____

Bigger Than Big!

Read this information about the biggest living thing. Think about the meanings of the words in bold type.

What is the biggest living thing? If you think the answer is a whale, you're wrong. The biggest living thing is the giant **sequoia.** Nothing in the animal **kingdom** comes close to the size of this evergreen tree. The blue whale can weigh 150 tons (140 metric tons). A giant sequoia weighs 20 times as much—3,000 tons (2,650 metric tons)!

The giant sequoia is tall. Many grow to a height of 250 feet (75 meters) or more. Yet other trees are taller. A Douglas fir, for example, can reach a height of 300 feet (90 meters). It is the **combination** of height and weight that makes the giant sequoia the biggest living thing. The Douglas fir has a thinner **trunk** than a giant sequoia. Therefore, it weighs much less. Many sequoias are 25 feet (7.5 meters) thick at the **base**. Some are more than 30 feet (9 meters) thick. This is about the **distance** from wall to wall in your classroom.

The biggest of all the giant sequoias is the General Sherman Tree. It grows in Sequoia National Park in California. It rises 272 feet (83 meters) above the forest floor. It has a diameter of 37 feet (11 meters). Its **circumference,** or distance around its base, is about 102 feet (35 meters). Scientists **estimate** that the tree weighs more than 6,100 tons (5,400 metric tons). There is enough wood in the General Sherman to build 40 five-room houses! Luckily, no one is going to build houses out of this tree. Most giant sequoias are protected in state or national parks.

98 ft.

A Tall Order

| Edit | Create | **Identify** |

Label
Find
Order

Label the drawing with the
correct vocabulary words.

sequoia combination
kingdom
trunk distance base
estimate circumference

98 ft.

_____

_____

_____

_____

Also...

1. Name another *kingdom* besides the animal kingdom.
2. *Estimate* the height of a tree in your neighborhood.
3. Find out the *distance* between Sequoia National Park
   and your city or town.
4. Find a synonym for *combination*.

73   Vocabulary 3, SV6767-0

Name _____ Date _____

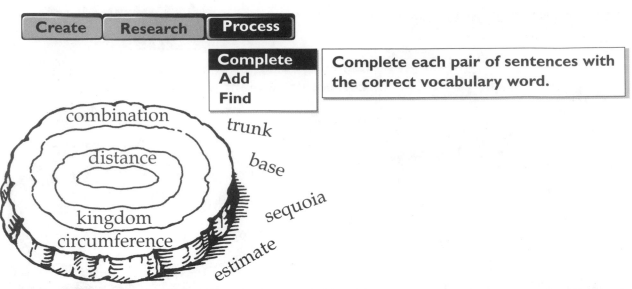

Complete
Add
Find

Complete each pair of sentences with the correct vocabulary word.

combination
trunk
distance
base
kingdom
sequoia
circumference
estimate

A Fine Pine

1. A maple sheds its leaves in the fall.
   A _____ keeps its leaves throughout the year.

2. You can add to find the exact total.
   You can _____ to find a rough total.

3. The diameter is the distance through the center of a circle.
   The _____ is the distance around a circle.

4. A plant has a stalk.
   A tree has a _____ .

5. The crown is the top of a tree.
   The _____ is the bottom of a tree.

Branching Out

1. Draw a map of California. Show the location of *Sequoia* National Park.
2. *Estimate* the distance between Sequoia National Park
   and Yosemite National Park.
3. What *combination* of events led to the establishment of national parks?
4. Name some other plants in the plant *kingdom*.

Unit IV Review

Synonyms are words that have the same or almost the same meaning. Choose a word from the word list that is a synonym for the word in bold type. Write it on the line. Read the sentence, using your choice, to check your work.

Word List

appetite	estimate	marsh	tentacles	species
lunges	combination	digest	creatures	stalks

_____ 1. There are many **kinds** of animals.

_____ 2. An octopus has eight **arms**.

_____ 3. The football player **jumps** for the ball.

_____ 4. My aunt has a big **hunger** and loves to cook.

_____ 5. Can you **calculate** the sum of 360 and 720?

_____ 6. Your body takes several hours to **absorb** food.

_____ 7. Grasses and other plants grow in the **swamp**.

_____ 8. Many unusual **animals** live in a rain forest.

_____ 9. Brass is a **union** of copper and zinc.

_____ 10. The world's biggest flower grows on the **stems** of wild grape vines.

Name _____ Date _____

Choose a word from the Word List that has the opposite meaning of the word or words in bold type. Write it on the line. Read the sentence to see if it makes more sense!

Word List				
estimate	combination	common	jungle	sense
adult	sensitive	escape	base	aggressive

_____ 11. I was worried that some of the ants would **remain in** the ant colony in my room.

_____ 12. She was afraid of that **timid** dog.

_____ 13. I have seen that kind of dog many times; it is a **rare** breed.

_____ 14. James sunburns easily because he has such **tough** skin.

_____ 15. You cannot go into that museum without **child** supervision.

_____ 16. There are many colorful birds and animals in the **desert**.

_____ 17. It just makes **confusion** when you bring your umbrella on a rainy day.

_____ 18. We can only **tell you exactly** how many stars there are in the sky.

_____ 19. The roots grow out of the **top** of the tree.

_____ 20. That **single** dance step had my feet all tangled up!

-The World's Most Popular Sport-

Read the information about a team sport. Think about the meanings of the words in bold type.

What is the world's most popular sport? The answer may surprise you. It's not baseball nor football. It's soccer! More people play it than any other sport. The game is especially popular in Europe and South America. Why do people like soccer? **Spectators** like it because it is exciting, and the **pace** is fast. The only time the game stops is when someone **scores**. Players like it because the **rules** are fairly simple. Also, you don't need much **equipment**. All you need is a ball.

Like football there are 2 teams. Each team has 11 players. The players try to get a ball into the other team's **goal**. The goal cages are at opposite ends of a playing field. Unlike football, only goalkeepers can touch the ball with their hands. Other players have to kick it with their feet. They can also use other parts of their bodies. Players can even hit the ball with their heads! When a team gets the ball into the goal, they score a point. The team with more goals wins.

People have been playing games like soccer for hundreds of years. The **ancient** Romans played with a ball filled with hair. In the 1100s, English players chased a ball made from a pig's bladder. Sometimes there were 100 or more players on a team. The games were often so rough that several kings tried to keep people from playing them. But they never **succeeded** in stopping the games. In the 1600s, Native Americans played a game called pasuckquakkohowog. The name means, "They gather to play ball with the foot." Each team had from 40 to 1,000 players. Can you imagine what it was like to keep score?

Kick it Around!

Edit	Create	**Identify**

Label
Order
Find

Label the drawing with the correct vocabulary words.

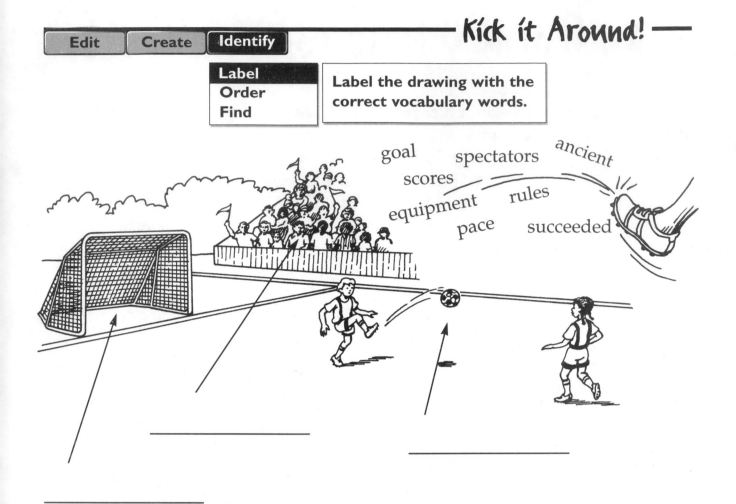

goal   spectators   ancient
scores
equipment   rules
pace   succeeded

_____

_____   _____

_____   _____

"Remember! You can't touch the ball with your hands. You have to kick it with your feet!"

Also...

Imagine you are the sports editor for your school newspaper. Write an article about a soccer match. Be sure to tell the *who, what, where, when, why,* and *how* in your article. Use the words *pace, scores, ancient,* and *succeeded* in your sentences. Write a headline for your article.

Create   Apply   **Process**

Classify
Label
Find

Classify the vocabulary words. Write the word that belongs in each group.

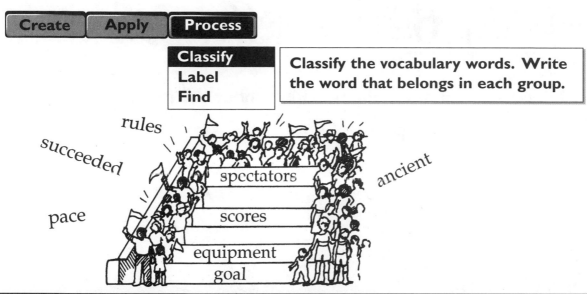

rules
succeeded
pace
spectators
scores
equipment
goal
ancient

Use Your Head!

1. guides, orders, _____
2. fans, viewers, _____
3. home plate, finish line, _____
4. tools, instruments, _____
5. speed, rate, _____
6. wins, records, _____
7. accomplished, completed, _____
8. old, out of date, _____

Keeping Score

Compare the 2 sports.	Football	Soccer
Number of players		
Equipment		
Object of game		
Length of game		
Method of scoring		

Name _____   Date _____

By the Beautiful Sea

Read this information about a hobby. Think about the meanings of the words in bold type.

Collecting things can be a great hobby. If you live near the ocean, you can collect shells. Shells are the homes of animals called **mollusks**. Some mollusks live in a shell that is shaped like a cone. They are called **univalves**. Other mollusks, called **bivalves**, have two shells. The shells are joined by a hinge. They can open and shut like a book.

Unlike some hobbies, shell collecting is not **expensive**. All you need is a **mesh** bag for carrying your shells. Mesh will let water drip out. Of course, if you want to look under the water for shells, you need a mask or goggles.

You don't have to wait for summer to start your collection. You can look for shells at any time of year. The best place to look is on a sandy beach. Shells **vary** from beach to beach. On New England beaches, you can pick up clam and scallop shells. On Florida beaches, you can find cockles, cowries, and conches. On California beaches, you can pick up murex and abalone shells.

Be sure to dry your shells in sand, not sun. Then grease them with a light oil such as salad oil. This will help **preserve** them. If you brush them with oil every few weeks, the colors will stay bright for years.

Shell collecting can be fun. Who knows! You may be lucky enough to find a Glory-of-the-Sea. This shell is worth about $20,000!

Name _____ Date _____

Edit | Create | **Identify**

Label
Match
Define

Label the drawing with the correct vocabulary words.

collecting
univalves   mollusks
expensive   bivalves
mesh   vary
preserve

Also...

How fast can you say the sentence, *"She sells seashells by the seashore"*? The sentence is called a tongue twister. Write your own tongue twisters. Use the words *collecting, expensive,* and *vary.* Write each word in a sentence. Begin as many words as you can with the same letter as the vocabulary word.

Name _____ Date _____

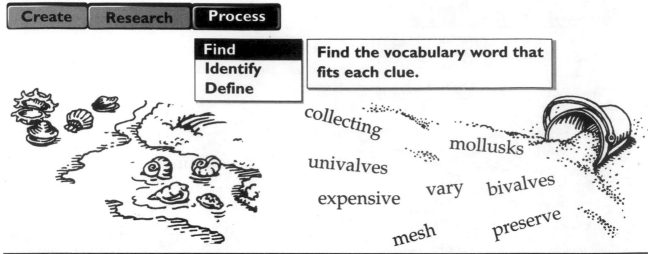

collecting

mollusks

univalves

expensive   vary   bivalves

mesh   preserve

Shell Shenanigans

_____   1. change

_____   2. animals with a soft body and a hard shell

_____   3. having a high price

_____   4. animals with a shell that has two parts
joined together

_____   5. gathering together

_____   6. protect

_____   7. a material with many open spaces

_____   8. animals having a one-piece shell

Create a picture by connecting the vocabulary words in ABC
order. Then write the words in ABC order.

univalves   vary   bivalves   collecting

preserve

expensive

mollusks   mesh

1. _____   5. _____

2. _____   6. _____

3. _____   7. _____

4. _____   8. _____

Bicycle's Golden Age

Read this story about bicycles. Think about the meanings of the words in bold type.

Between 1890 and 1900, a bicycle **craze** swept over America. Everyone rode a bike. Bankers and stage stars took to the sport. Almost every town and city had a bicycle club. The clubs held races, **tours**, and picnics. Some held "dances" where riders pedaled around a ballroom to waltz music.

Why was **cycling** so popular? First of all it was fun. Women loved to ride! It gave them a taste of freedom. Many doctors told people to cycle. They thought it cured headaches. Cycling was also a cheap way to travel. Before the bicycle, people rode on horseback. However, not everyone had the money to buy a horse. Many of those who could **afford** one had no place to keep it. Bikes, on the other hand, could be stored almost anywhere.

Not everyone was happy with the craze. Watchmakers grumbled. Parents were buying bikes, not watches, for their children's birthdays. Candy makers were upset. Many children stopped buying candy. They were saving their pennies to buy leather seats and handle grips.

Horses were another problem. They were afraid of the new **contraption**. If a horse reared and broke something, the cyclist had to pay to fix it. Because of the danger to horses, cyclists could not ride on paths in Central Park in New York City. In New Jersey, cyclists could not ride on highways or **turnpikes**.

The bicycle craze lasted until the early 1900s. Then Americans found a new love—the **automobile**. This new **transportation** owed a lot to the bicycle. Cyclists had fought for better roads and had gotten them. They also had won the right to ride wherever they liked. Turnpikes opened their gates to bikes. Now they welcomed cars. America had become a nation on wheels!

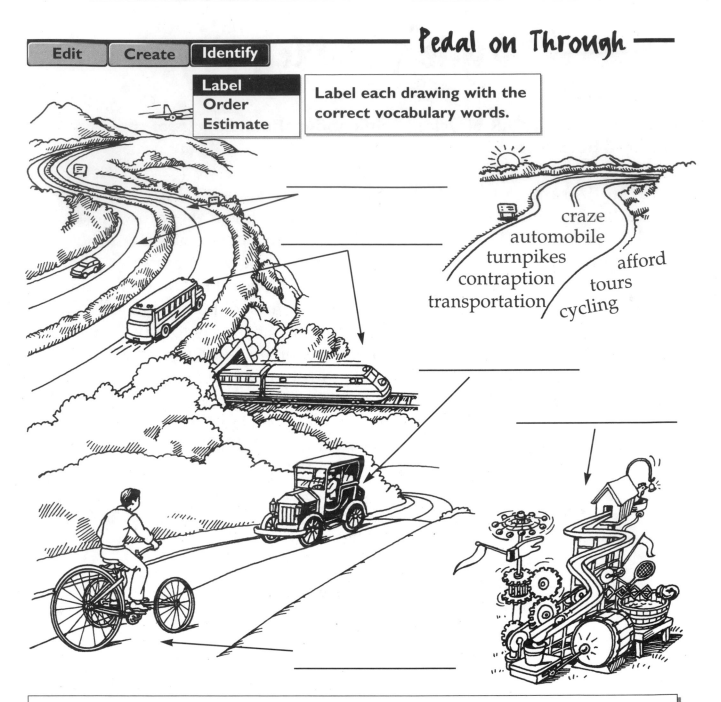

Edit **Create** **Identify**

Label
Order
Estimate

Label each drawing with the
correct vocabulary words.

craze
automobile
turnpikes
contraption
transportation
afford
tours
cycling

Also...

In the 1890s, some people loved bicycles. Others did not. Imagine that you
lived at the turn of the century. How would you have felt about bicycles?
Write a letter to the editor of your local newspaper. Explain why bicycles
should or should not be allowed on roads and highways. Use the words
afford, *tours*, and *craze* in your sentences.

Name _____ Date _____

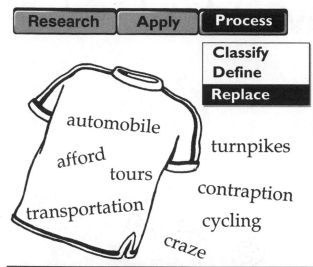

Replace the word or words in bold type with a vocabulary word.

automobile
afford
tours
transportation
turnpikes
contraption
cycling
craze

Keep Your Balance

1. Albert Pope started the bicycle **short-lived fashion** in America. _____
2. He saw the **gadget** at a show in Philadelphia in 1876. _____
3. He loved the new **means of moving people.** _____
4. Pope thought that Americans would like **riding bicycles.** _____
5. He made a bicycle that most people could **have enough money to buy.** _____
6. People pedaled his "Columbia" on **trips** through the countryside. _____

Car-rumba!

Find the information you need to complete the following exercises.

1. Draw a picture of an *automobile.*
2. Find a road map of your state. Label the *turnpikes.*

Let's Go Fly a Kite!

Read this story about kites. Think about the meanings of the words in bold type.

What's a fun thing to do on a windy day? Fly a kite, of course. You can make your own kite. The two-stick or diamond kite is easy to make. All you need are two sticks, some glue, paper, and strips of cloth. First, tie the sticks together to make a cross. Then cover the **frame** with paper. Tie a string to each end of one stick. Tie another string to the ends of the other stick. **Attach** a longer string where the two strings cross. Be sure to glue cloth strips to the end of the frame. They serve as the kite's tail. Without it, your kite will crash to the ground!

Now, you'll need a place to fly your kite. Look for an open space with good winds. A beach, a meadow, a field, and a park are all good kite-flying **areas**. Never fly your kite near an airport. It's dangerous, and it's against the law! Never fly your kite during a thunderstorm. Lightning could strike you!

You have wind, a kite, and a place to fly it. Now how do you get your kite up in the air? **Launching** is easy—once you know how. Hold the kite high over your head. Toss it upwards into the wind. As the wind flows past the kite, a force called **lift** is created. This force makes the kite rise into the sky. As the kite goes higher, let out, or **release**, more line. Don't let the kite **sag**. Keep the string tight, but not too tight. This takes practice.

Landing a kite also takes practice. Walk toward the kite. This will take the pressure off the line. Then **reel** in the line. Your kite will float gently to a safe landing. You'll be ready for another windy day!

Name _____   Date _____

Edit	Create	**Identify**

Label
Match
Define

Label the drawing with the
correct vocabulary words.

attach   frame
areas   launching
release
lift
reel
sag

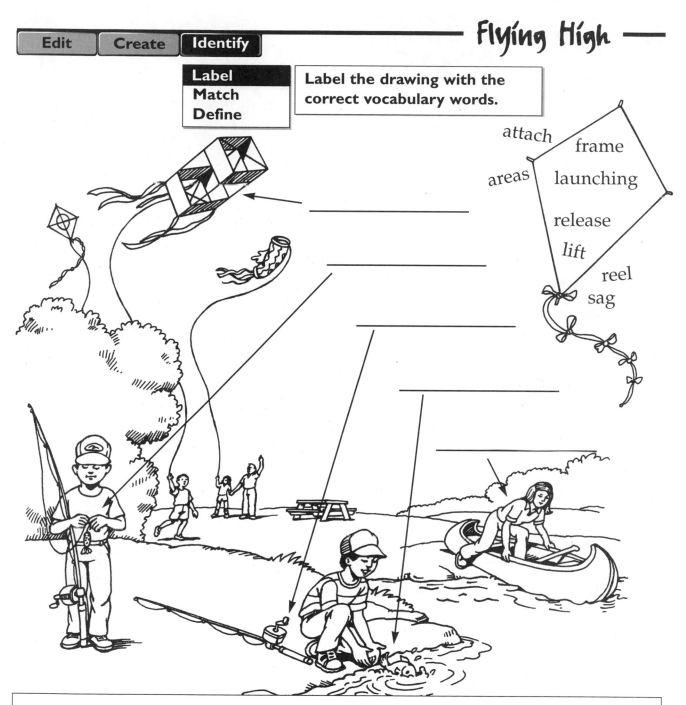

_____

_____

_____

_____

_____

Also...

Find the vocabulary word that contains, or is contained in, each word. Use each vocabulary word in a sentence.

1. are
2. passage
3. Draw a picture to demonstrate the word *lift*.

Name _____ Date _____

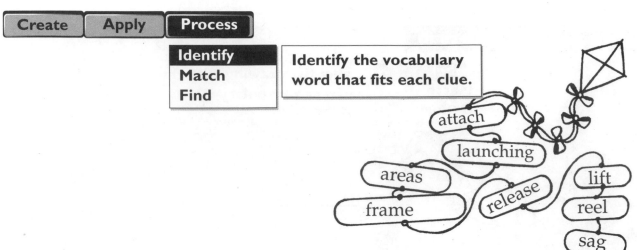

Create   Apply   **Process**

Identify
Match
Find

Identify the vocabulary
word that fits each clue.

attach
launching
areas
frame
release
lift
reel
sag

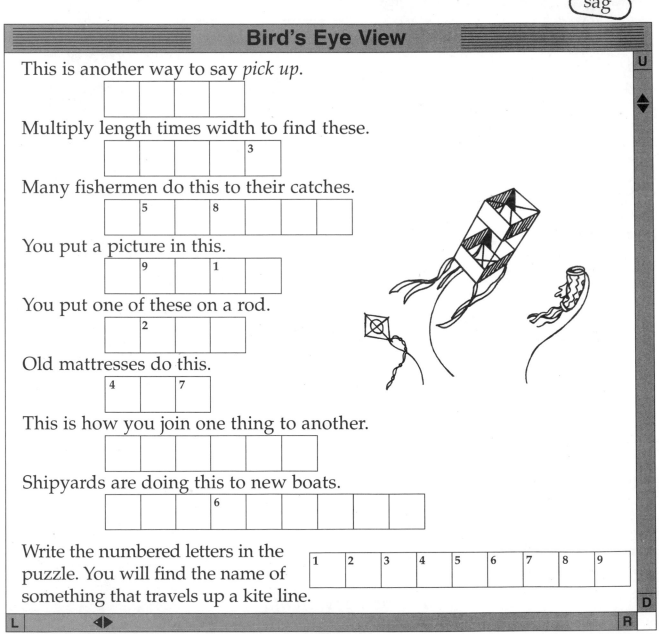

Bird's Eye View

This is another way to say *pick up*.

Multiply length times width to find these.

Many fishermen do this to their catches.

You put a picture in this.

You put one of these on a rod.

Old mattresses do this.

This is how you join one thing to another.

Shipyards are doing this to new boats.

Write the numbered letters in the
puzzle. You will find the name of
something that travels up a kite line.

1	2	3	4	5	6	7	8	9

Skating...In-Line!

Read this information about rollerblading. Think about the meanings of the words in bold type.

Who invented **skates**? No one really knows. What we do know is that people first skated on ice! Long ago someone put sharp **splinters** of animal bone on the bottom of a pair of boots. These were the first ice skates. Later, wood took the place of bone. About 700 years ago, people skated on frozen **canals** in Holland. In 1760, Joseph Merlin figured out how to skate when there was no ice. He put wooden **spools** on the **soles** of his shoes. His skates were never popular. Skaters found it too hard to stop.

Inventors kept trying to make a better skate. In the early 1800s, Robert Tyers put 5 wheels in a line on a pair of shoes. Most people thought his device was silly. Then, in 1863, John Plimpton had a different design. He put a pair of wheels in front and another pair in back. Soon everyone was roller skating.

The idea of in-line skates did not fade away. In-line skating is more like ice skating than roller skating. So skaters kept **tinkering** with an in-line design. In 1980, 2 brothers from Minnesota found an old in-line skate in a sports shop. The Olson brothers thought hockey players would like them. Players wouldn't need ice rinks. They could train on concrete and **asphalt**.

The Olsons set up shop in their parents' home. They put wheels in a line on a pair of boots. The boots were padded and fit like ski boots. For stopping, they put a brake pad on the **heel** of the right skate. Hockey players bought them as fast as the Olsons made them! Skiers also began using them. Now people all across the country are rolling . . . in-line!

Name _____   Date _____

| Edit | Create | Identify |

Label
Classify
Estimate

Label the drawing with the correct vocabulary words.

skates
soles
splinters
tinkering
asphalt   heel
canals
spools

Also...

Picture the words *splinters*, *tinkering*, *canals*, and *asphalt*. Write the words to show their meaning. Here is an example.

Name _____ Date _____

Research | Apply | Process

Replace
Add
Identify

Replace the word or words in bold type with a vocabulary word.

soles   skates   tinkering
splinters   heel
canals   asphalt   spools

Great Skating

1. Would you like to skate on **pieces of broken bone**? _____

2. Skating on wooden **cylinders** was not easy. _____

3. The wheels were attached to the **bottoms** of shoes. _____

4. A roller skate has no brake pad on the **lower back**. _____

5. With wheels, you can skate on **concrete**. _____

6. Inventors keep **playing** with the design. _____

Get In-Line!

Draw a picture of a new in-line or roller skate. Explain why your skate is better than older models.

Name _____ Date _____

Unit V Review

Read each meaning. Fill in the bubble beside the word that fits the meaning.

1. sharp, thin pieces
   - ○ contraption
   - ○ spools
   - ○ splinters

2. having a high price
   - ○ craze
   - ○ expensive
   - ○ automobile

3. the means of moving something from one place to another
   - ○ transportation
   - ○ spectators
   - ○ turnpikes

4. had a good result
   - ○ varied
   - ○ launched
   - ○ succeeded

5. set free
   - ○ release
   - ○ tinker
   - ○ preserve

6. trips in which many places are visited
   - ○ canals
   - ○ skates
   - ○ tours

7. keep from decaying
   - ○ frame
   - ○ preserve
   - ○ succeed

8. making minor repairs
   - ○ tinkering
   - ○ collecting
   - ○ launching

9. things that are needed for a purpose
   - ○ tours
   - ○ equipment
   - ○ scores

10. send forcefully up or out
    - ○ pace
    - ○ sag
    - ○ launch

Name _____ Date _____

Use two words from the Word List to fill in the blanks of the story.

		Word List		
asphalt	afford	attach	ancient	expensive
collecting	release	scores	canals	craze

Sports have been around since **11.** _____ times. For some people,

the **12.** _____ are the most important thing in sports. But many

people play just for the fun of it. Many people have hobbies that center around

13. _____ cards of famous sports figures. The cards with the

most famous athletes on them can be very **14.** _____ . Some

sports start out as a **15.** _____ that not many people can

16. _____ . As time goes on, they become very common.

Some sports require many people to form teams. Others, like fishing, can be

done alone. All you need to do is **17.** _____ a worm to your

hook, throw it into the water, and enjoy the peace and quiet around you.

Though fishing can be a way to catch dinner, many people fish just for the

fun of it. They **18.** _____ the fish back into the water.

Skating is a sport that has been around for a long, long time. People began ice

skating on the **19.** _____ in winter. Now in-line skating is even

more popular. Skaters can be found almost anywhere there is

20. _____ ! One thing we can be sure of is that there will always

be sports to play and new and exciting ways to play them.

Vocabulary List

active	dune	machine	sequoia
adult	electricity	manufacture	shallow
afford	elevators	marshes	signs
aggressive	encyclopedia	material	skates
alphabetical	energy	mesh	skyline
ancient	enormous	microscope	skyscrapers
appetites	equipment	molecules	soles
architect	escape	mollusks	solid
areas	estimate	moons	spacecraft
asphalt	events	mucus	spared
attach	expands	narrow	species
automobile	expedition	navigate	spectators
avoid	expensive	oval	spine
barometer	explore	pace	splinters
base	fabric	particles	spools
bivalves	facts	pattern	stalks
breeds	fears	permanent	still
broadcasting	female	pigments	stories
canals	fiberglass	planets	substance
cells	follicle	plankton	succeeded
charts	forecasts	poison ivy	suction
circumference	frame	pollen	surface
clusters	gases	ponds	surrounded
collecting	glaciers	popular	surveying
combination	goal	possessive	tailor
common	healthy	precipitation	telegraph
compact disks	heel	preserve	telescope
concentrate	height	pressure	television
construction	horizon	probably	temperature
contact	huge	protecting	tentacles
continent	improved	radio	thunder
contraption	indirectly	rank	tinkering
control	information	rash	tons
craters	ingredients	reactions	topics
craze	insects	receiver	tours
creatures	instrument	reel	trachea
cycling	insulator	regular	transportation
dangerous	interior	relax	trapdoor
depends	invented	release	trunk
depressions	irritates	resist	turnpikes
deserts	jellyfish	root	univalves
design	jungle	rules	vary
designed	key word	sacs	vegetation
device	kingdom	sag	vibrates
diameter	lake	scalp	vocal cords
digests	launching	scientists	volts
directly	lift	scores	volume
disappear	lightning	seams	voyage
discover	liquid	sense	weather
distance	lunges	sensitive	weighs

Answer Key
Vocabulary Grade 3

P.6/7/8
Assessment Test
1. vibrate
2. pressure
3. construction
4. device
5. design
6. suction
7. launching
8. afford
9. reaction
10. topic
11. surrounded
12. temperature
13. particle
14. manufacture
15. diameter
16. discover
17. ancient
18. univalve
19. volume
20. expedition

P.11
1. topics
2. facts
3. encyclopedia
4. key word
5. spine
6. volume

P.14
ACROSS:
1. active
4. reactions
7. probably
8. depends
DOWN:
2. concentrate
3. regular
5. relax
6. events

P.16
Also...
1. narrow
2. pigments
3. oval
4. permanent

P.17
1. narrow
2. oval
3. scalp
4. root
5. permanent
6. cells
7. pigments
8. follicle

P.20
1. healthy
2. trachea
3. vocal cords
4. control
5. pollen
6. irritates
7. signs
8. mucus

P.23
contact
avoid
rash
clusters
directly
PUZZLE:
urushiol

P.24/25
Unit I Review
1. healthy
2. permanent
3. indirectly
4. narrow
5. avoid
6. irritate
7. relax
8. contact
9. root
10. concentrate
11. alphabetical
12. spine
13. relax
14. probably
15. oval
16. pollen
17. vocal cords
18. clusters
19. rash
20. volume

P.28
ACROSS:
1. temperature
3. enormous
4. interior
7. vegetation
8. deserts
DOWN:
2. precipitation
5. scientists
6. dune

P.30
Also...
1. invented
2. pressure

P.31
1. barometer
2. instrument
3. telegraph
4. information
5. weather
6. invented
7. pressure
8. forecasts

P.33
Also...
1. voyage
2. surveying
3. expedition

P.34
continent
voyage
horizon
explore
surveying
charts
navigate
expedition
PUZZLE:
Endeavor

P.37
1. thunder
2. electricity
3. dangerous
4. volts
5. lightning
6. expands
7. energy
8. vibrates

P.39
Also...
1. shallow
2. disappear

P.40
1. shallow
2. glaciers
3. craters
4. ponds
5. lake

P.41/42
Unit II Review
1. precipitation
2. information
3. invented
4. volts
5. glaciers
6. explore
7. dangerous
8. interior
9. disappear
10. voyage
11. dune
12. enormous
13. navigate
14. continent
15. pressure
16. depression
17. weather
18. interior
19. vegetation
20. charts

P.45
1. skyline
2. skyscrapers
3. elevators
4. designed
5. architect
6. stories
7. height
8. construction

P.48
ACROSS:
2. solid
6. spacecraft
7. surface
8. moons
DOWN:
1. telescope
3. particles
4. gases
5. planets

P.51
1. receiver
2. still
3. device
4. television
5. improved
6. radio
7. broadcasting
8. pattern

P.54
1. liquid
2. ingredients
3. molecules
4. material
5. microscope
6. fiberglass
7. insulator
8. resist

P.57
1. fabric
2. huge
3. manufacture
4. popular
5. seams
6. tailor
7. machine
8. spared

95

Vocabulary 3, SV6767-0

P.58/59
Unit III Review
1. planet
2. liquid
3. architect
4. machine
5. television
6. telescope
7. skyscrapers
8. huge
9. pattern
10. insulator
11. architect
12. designed
13. surface
14. moon
15. radio
16. resist
17. huge
18. popular
19. stories
20. skyline

P.62
1. breeds
2. rank
3. possessive
4. aggressive
5. protecting
6. lunges
7. escape
8. discover

P.65
1. diameter
2. female
3. common
4. design

P.68
1. insects
2. stalks
3. marshes
4. trapdoor
5. sensitive
6. sacs
7. digests
8. suction
Don't Feed...
1. insects
2. trapdoor
3. digests
4. suction

P.71
species
adult
sense
weighs
fears
appetites
PUZZLE:
plants

P.74
1. sequoia
2. estimate
3. circumference
4. trunk
5. base

P.75/76
Unit IV Review
1. species
2. tentacles
3. lunges
4. appetite
5. estimate
6. digest
7. marsh
8. creatures
9. combination
10. stalks
11. escape
12. aggressive
13. common
14. sensitive
15. adult
16. jungle
17. sense
18. estimate
19. base
20. combination

P.79
1. rules
2. spectators
3. goal
4. equipment
5. pace
6. scores
7. succeeded
8. ancient

P.82
1. vary
2. mollusks
3. expensive
4. bivalves
5. collecting
6. preserve
7. mesh
8. univalves

P.85
1. craze
2. contraption
3. transportation
4. cycling
5. afford
6. tours

P.87
Also...
1. areas
2. sag

P.88
lift
areas
release
frame
reel
sag
attach
launching
PUZZLE:
messenger

P.91
1. splinters
2. spools
3. soles
4. heel
5. asphalt
6. tinkering

P.92/93
Unit V Review
1. splinters
2. expensive
3. transportation
4. succeeded
5. release
6. tours
7. preserve
8. tinkering
9. equipment
10. launch
11. ancient
12. scores
13. collecting
14. expensive
15. craze
16. afford
17. attach
18. release
19. canals
20. asphalt